DARREN GOUGH'S
BOOK FOR YOUNG CRICKETERS

DARREN GOUGH'S

BOOK FOR YOUNG CRICKETERS

My Guide to Your Success

Darren Gough

WITH

David Hopps

Hodder & Stoughton

To my mum and dad, Trevor and Christine,
for the early years when they gave up so much.

To my wife Anna and son Liam whose love and support have
done so much to improve my life and career.

Finally, to Wayne Morton, the Yorkshire and England physio,
for his non-stop encouragement and advice during my ups and
downs. (A great man.)

Copyright © 1996 by Darren Gough

First published in Great Britain by
Hodder & Stoughton
a division of Hodder Headline PLC

The right of Darren Gough to be identified as the author of
this work has been asserted by him in accordance with the
Copyright, Designs and Patents Act 1988.

10 9 8 7 6 5 4 3 2 1

A CIP catalogue record for this title is available
from the British Library

ISBN 0 340 66627 7

Design and computer page make up
Tony & Penny Mills

Printed in Great Britain by
Mackays of Chatham PLC

Hodder and Stoughton Ltd
A Division of Hodder Headline PLC
338 Euston Road
London NW1 3BH

Contents

Foreword

In my view, Darren Gough is a BAD cricketer. Before the Yorkie lynch mob come looking for me, let me explain.

Not bad as in hopeless, laughable, useless, the opposite of good, etc., but B-A-D as in *Belief, Ability* and *Desire.*

These are the three main components that make up any truly outstanding cricketer. If you possess enough of one of the above, you might have a chance of being considered a moderate player and a reasonable amount of two of them will produce a fairly good competitor.

But when all three are present they add up to the potential for greatness. Darren has them and in abundance.

When I watched Darren take his first steps in international cricket, against the touring Kiwis and South Africans in 1994, and then Down Under that winter, what struck me first was his self-belief. Unlike some young players I could mention, he entered the stage as though he was convinced he belonged there.

His ability to swing the ball at pace, and swing it over the boundary with relish when batting, soon became clear. And his desire shone through the gloom at the Sydney Cricket Ground when he first smashed a brilliant 51 to get England out of trouble, then ripped through the Aussies to take 6 for 49 in the first innings of the third Ashes Test.

These were performances that suggested Darren was on the road to the top. Sadly for him and England, the injury that struck him down and out of the last two Tests in Australia has dogged his efforts to take the next steps. But I have been mightily impressed by his refusal to view what has befallen him during the past year as anything other than a temporary setback.

With luck and careful handling, Darren will be back and blazing, belief and ability intact, and the desire within him burning even more brightly.

Ian Botham

7

1   It's Your Life

It's your life – and it might seem a million miles away from that of an international cricketer. The thrills and excitement triggered by playing cricket for England could well be something that you can only dream about. What good, you might be wondering, can Darren Gough do for me? You'd be surprised!

Even if I don't play another Test match, I've no hesitation in saying that I've been tremendously lucky. Just to pull on a sweater bearing England's three lions was a moment to remember for the rest of my life. The rest has been a wonderful bonus. I've shivered with pleasure when a crowd bursts into applause at something I've done on the field. I've been exuberant about the good times, wistful over the bad, and I've relished the merriment that should always be part of playing sport for your country.

Those of you blessed with a special talent might one day, with good fortune and a lot of hard work, sample the elation that top-level sport can bring. I'd love you to follow in my footsteps. It is a rewarding life.

The majority of people, of course, will have to accept something less. When I left school in Barnsley at sixteen, there was not exactly much evidence to hand that I was about to make a mark.

But don't assume that all the joys of playing cricket are reserved entirely for those who reach the top. Don't abandon the game at the first sign of failure. With the right attitude, everybody's cricket experiences can be immensely rewarding. I want to help you discover how.

If people praise me for anything, it is because I have communicated my pleasure of playing cricket for a living. They like the fact that I seem so cheery and buoyant on the field. If they have endured another humdrum day, I might even give them a bit of a lift. That is something that makes me tremendously proud. Sure, I like a laugh and a joke. There is no reason for me to be embarrassed about it. I don't see why I should have a humour bypass operation just because I'm in the middle of a Test match.

The ancient Yorkshire cricketer, Emmott Robinson, who once remarked, 'We don't play this game for fun,' might have had a problem or two with me. He was right up to a point. Professional sport is played to win, more so now than at any time in our history. But that is no reason to frown upon those of us who are determined to enjoy it along the way.

I'm convinced that my arrival in the England team has, for whatever reason, coincided with a new, more upbeat attitude. A new generation of players is determined that, unlike some teams in the recent past, they will not be worn down by the all-consuming pressures caused by non-stop TV and newspaper attention, but will try to relish every moment that they are in the spotlight. We will also be striving to make England the best and most entertaining team in the world.

Every one of you can help me to spread that positive attitude throughout the country. Wherever you play cricket – whether it is at school, a scruffy recreation ground, an idyllic village setting, an ambitious club side, or in a representative eleven – make it your aim both to play to the peak of your potential and have maximum enjoyment along the way.

I'm determined that *Darren Gough's Book For Young Cricketers* will show you how to tap your potential. Sadly, many young players never stretch their ability to the limit. They suspect that it is not worth the effort, that it will all become too much like hard work.

Well, ask yourself this. Do I look like I am not enjoying myself? Would I rather still be playing for my first village side, Monk Bretton, near Barnsley, or performing in front of a packed crowd in a Lord's Test? Monk Bretton gave me an excellent grounding, but there's only one answer!

Maximising your potential can at the same time maximise your enjoyment. There is endless pleasure to be had in trying to play cricket properly – in improving your fitness, understanding the basic technical demands of the game, the mental as well as the physical battle, and in learning how to approach properly every game you play. Whatever level you reach, if you know that you have done the best that you can, you have every right to feel proud.

It is high time that we declared war upon the moaners and the groaners, or the young players on the skive, or the miserable old-timers who don't give a damn about the next generation, all of whom will be playing long after they have retired, or the

Don't let people tell you that cricket is a dog's life. My Jack Russell, Jack, would never believe it.

cheats who don't care about the traditions of a great game. I wouldn't give any of them the time of day, and there's no good reason why you should either.

At any level, there is no future in slouching through a game, not really caring how you perform, or whether you win or lose. Enthusiasm is one of the greatest gifts a cricketer can give to the game. Life only gives you one chance, so in whatever you are doing, you might as well give it your best shot.

To guide you along the way, I've even called in the assistance of my England team-mates, who have provided their own special tips on how to improve your game. I've also tried to give you a taste of life at the top, with chapters about my life playing cricket for Yorkshire and for England. There were times when I was close to packing the game up, and finding other employment. But I stuck at it, and will always be thankful that I did.

Relish the opportunities that youth and sport bring you, and play your cricket as spiritedly as you can. At its best, cricket is a great game. I hope I can help you discover some of its secrets.

Enjoy yourself and good luck,

The Dazzler.

2 It's My Life

According to the media, I've been a strapping England hero and a tubby Yorkshire flop; a player heading for instant stardom, or heading for the sack. One minute I'm a breath of fresh air, the next minute I'm in danger of becoming a buffoon. It's all part of being a professional sportsman. Life is always colourful in the wacky world of newspapers.

◆ *'He is highly rated and clearly appreciates the value of a good length.'*
John Callaghan, accurately predicting my Yorkshire debut in the *Yorkshire Evening Post*, 1989.

◆ *'There is a hint in Gough of another South Yorkshire seam bowler, Graham Stevenson, in that slightly ruffled, unabashed air, a casual stroll in the outfield, and a head tipped slightly skywards on his approach to the crease.'*
David Hopps (my co-author in this book), in the *Yorkshire Post*, describing my debut against Middlesex, 1989. At least the Stevo comparison made a change from Ian Botham.

◆ *'Australia beware – there's another budding Botham straining to sink his teeth into you. While Ian the Invincible may be past the peak of his powers, a new young firebrand has already chiselled out his first foothold on the long haul to the summit. And he's determined to trample his way to the top in the same buccaneering manner that established his mentor as Aussie cricket's public enemy no. 1.'*
John Edwards, *Daily Mirror*, 1989, wasting no time in drawing those Botham comparisons!

◆ *'A likeable member of Yorkshire's team who is not afraid to put his back into his work and whose cheerful disposition is an added bonus after the surly years.'*
Martin Searby, in complimentary mood in the *Sheffield Star Green 'Un*, my local Saturday night sports paper, 1989.

◆ *'On this form Gough should be a crowd-puller in the Ian Botham mould.'*
Robert Mills, in the *Yorkshire Post*, after my whirlwind 72 against Leicestershire at Grace Road – my first senior appearance of the 1991 season.

◆ *'Darren Gough did little to justify the high hopes held for him.'*
John Callaghan, in the 1991 *Wisden*, far from confident about my first-class future.

◆ *'The razzmatazz of the county game seemed to have him trapped. Although he has always had a keen interest in his cricket, his concentration on the job in hand has often been distracted by cameras, big crowds and general media interest. Any little gimmicks or crazes would attract his attention. Coloured clothing, coloured sun creams and sunglasses easily caught his eye.'*
Phil Carrick, my first Yorkshire skipper, offering an older man's counsel, in *Yorkshire on Sunday*, 1993. 'Fergie' was the first professional to tell me that I would play for England . . . in one-day cricket.

◆ *'He bowled some express deliveries in the match, but the most encouraging feature of his dynamic display was his ability to achieve a rich and varied mixture in terms of pace and length.'*
Robert Mills again, upon my breakthrough match, Yorkshire's championship game against Somerset at Taunton, 1993.

◆ *'Gough suddenly seems to have discovered the ability to bowl very straight.'*
John Callaghan in the *Yorkshire Evening Post*, beginning to be impressed, near the end of the 1993 season.

◆ *'Keep an eye on Gough. Fast bowling is hard work, but the Yorkshire youngster looks to have great potential.'*
Richie Benaud, *News of the World*, 1993.

◆ *'Like Botham, Gough is a habitual experimenter. A single over is likely to develop into an impromptu variety show as he is overtaken by a desire to bowl every ball in his repertoire, as well as those which still exist only in his imagination.'*
David Hopps, in the *Guardian*, 1993, marking my call-up for the England A tour of South Africa.

◆ *'Gough is from F. S. Trueman country, more or less, and has something of his predecessor's stockiness.'*
Comparison with another great name from the past, this time in a learned piece by Michael Henderson in *The Times*, England's A tour of South Africa, 1994.

◆ *'Not since Graham Dilley burst on to the international scene fourteen years ago have I seen an Englishman burst with such pace and control.'*
Jon Agnew, BBC Radio cricket correspondent in the *Daily Express* after my successful one-day debut at Edgbaston, 1994.

◆ *'Darren Gough's future as an England cricketer began to take recognisable shape the day he turned his nose up at a hamburger.'*
Peter Johnson, *Daily Mail*, on my junk food habit, 1994.

◆ *'Living proof of the saying, "behind every successful man is a good woman."'*
Graham Otway, in *Today*, dwelling on Anna's part in my rejection of junk food, 1994.

◆ *'As Yorkshire as a Barnsley chop.'*
John Etheridge, the *Sun*, 1994.

'As Yorkshire as a Barnsley chop.' Yorkshire's sights and sounds have always been very important to me.

◆ *'It is probably ten years – it only seems like a millennium – since the Test debut of an England fast bowler was awaited with the glow of anticipation that surrounds Darren Gough today.'*
Peter Johnson, *Daily Mail*, 1994.

◆ *'It's not so much what he does as the way that he does it. Debutants are supposed to be shy, retiring and nervous. Gough is brash, self-confident and cocky. His face gives everything away, for they are the looks of a cheeky chap who expects things to happen.'*
Robert Mills, *Yorkshire Post*, 1994.

◆ *'What he showed in his Test debut was not simply the ability to bowl fast or cleave about him to good effect with the bat, but an exuberance and a joy at being young and fit and playing cricket for a living that was infectious enough to engage even the most jaded spectator.'*
Michael Parkinson, *Daily Telegraph*.

◆ *'For God's sake don't let the England bowling coaches anywhere near him! They destroyed poor old Devon Malcolm – temporarily I hope – by trying to get him to bowl line and length instead of quick and nasty. The same must not be allowed to happen to Gough or they'll have to answer to me first and the whole nation next.'*
Ian Botham, in controversial mood, 1994.

◆ *'Gough's gumption has caught the imagination in Australia. They are used to their Poms being diffident and diplomatic, not brash and brimming with bravado like their own sportsmen.'*
Colin Bateman, *Daily Express*, during early days of my first senior tour, in Australia, 1994.

◆ *'There might be something homespun about Darren Gough, with kick-ass epithets emblazoned inside his pads and his block-and-bash self-deprecatory batting, but by golly the lad has spirit. Not to mention talent and personality.'*
Mike Selvey, the *Guardian*, after my half-century in the Sydney Test, 1995.

◆ *'The tour is rapidly becoming the Darren Gough roadshow and, as such, a passport to fame and fortune. But it has been well earned. His bowling here . . . was exemplary: fast, accurate, mature and gutsy.'*
Mike Selvey again, after I followed up with 6 for 49, my England best, as we narrowly failed to win the Sydney Test, 1995.

◆ *'Gough holds up his head, sticks out his chest – one suspects a
Union flag is tattooed upon it – and whistles as he sets foot on
a cricket field. His is the exuberance of the young milkman on
a sunny morning, though the friskiest of milkmen would stop
short of doing a handstand during his round, as Gough did in
the Test match at the Sydney Cricket Ground.'*
Scyld Berry, *Sunday Telegraph*, after my Sydney Test exploits,
1995.

◆ *'At the moment, Gough is the publicist's dream – talented,
photogenic, a natural actor and quick with the one-liners.'*
Peter Johnson, *Daily Mail*, in the wake of the Sydney Test, 1995.

◆ *'Funny, our Darren's always had that smile from a baby. Our
photo albums are just full up with them on every page.'*
My dad, Trevor, finding plenty to smile about himself during
the Sydney Test, 1995.

One of the
smiles from
Mum and Dad's
photo album!

◆ *'Don't allow people to have you running after every opportunity
to promote yourself. Don't jump at every chance of exposure.
You can have the world come to you and take your choices.'*
Gary Lineker's advice to me in the *Observer* after the adulation
during the Sydney Test. I was about to come down to earth with
a crash! 1995.

◆ *'The lad wi' nowt taken out.'*
Paul Weaver, the *Guardian*, 1995.

◆ *'He's done very well, has doo-da, but if you just look at any cricketer these days he cracks up.'*
Brian Close, Yorkshire's cricket chairman, upon my return from Australia with a fractured foot, 1995.

◆ *'He's from Barnsley, and in the Republic of South Yorkshire you don't get carried away by your own importance.'*
Chris Hassell, Yorkshire's chief executive, asked if my success in Australia would go to my head, 1995.

◆ *'Trueman and Boycott have done little to scupper stereotypes of Yorkshiremen. Both, brilliant sportsmen that they were, are blessed with a gauche truculence and are given to self-opinion-ated bluster. Gough is free of such impediments. His behaviour in public will do much to enhance England's perception of Yorkshire and what it takes to be a Yorkshireman.'*
Colin Brazier, *Yorkshire Post*, 1995.

◆ *'In danger of becoming a buffoon.'*
Robin Marlar, *Sunday Times*, as I struggled with injury during England's 1995 home series against the West Indies.

◆ *'Darren Gough and I have agreed that we must get together for the sake of Yorkshire and England.'*
Fred Trueman, famous Yorkshire and England fast bowler, vowing to help me rediscover my form, in the *Sunday People*, as I struggled in the first two Tests of the 1995–6 South Africa tour.

3 Dazzler's South Africa Diary

OCTOBER 1995

Wednesday 18th: departure day. As soon as I walk into the Excelsior Hotel, the business starts: interviews, photos, bat signing sessions, and the collection of the latest freebie, a Motorola mobile phone. All this activity fails to disguise the saddest time of the tour. It was hard to say goodbye to Anna, my wife, and Liam. Imagine that he was only born on the eve of the Brisbane Test last year. Once we leave Heathrow at 2100, there is every chance to reflect upon a hectic last year. I've got to work hard to get back into the Test side, but hopefully by the third Test things will be going well.

Thursday 19th: arrived in Johannesburg as part of England's first touring party to South Africa since 1965. Proud to be part of the new South Africa. Their media build up the tour as a contest between their bowlers and our batsmen, which led to a few fed-up English quicks! Our chief aim is to win the Test series, but if we can do anything in the townships, we'll be proud to be part of it. My first roomie is Graeme Hick. He's a quiet bloke, but a good man to sort you out early in the tour. The British vice-consul advises us on the dos and don'ts of Johannesburg.

Friday 20th: first net session cancelled, so Wayne Morton, our physio, introduced sprints instead – what he calls the Attitude Test. A hospitable evening at the Consul General's residence ended with Wayne and Ramble (Mark Ilott) playing guitars on stage. Not sure if the guests could believe it.

Saturday 21st: we're all issued with high-performance nutrition drinks (blackcurrant flavour). Also some of the boys, myself included, are trying Creatine, an energy booster which does not contravene any drug-testing regulations! Afternoon spent at the official opening of the new clubhouse in Alexandra township. There was a large turnout and Devon Malcolm said some encouraging words to the underprivileged kids. Dev can be a real role model here.

Sunday 22nd: Mizuno had given the lads eight sets of golf clubs for the tour, so after nets it was time to try them out. The only problem was that the pro shop was closed and we were limited to one ball each. That tested my accuracy!

Monday 23rd: nets deteriorating. A waste of time really. Had an afternoon golf date at the exclusive River Island club against Nicky Oppenheimer's XI. Thorpey (Graham Thorpe) and myself won first prize off a 17 handicap. Not surprisingly, people called us bandits. Informal dinner at the Oppenheimer residence in the evening – and what a residence!

Tuesday 24th: our first warm-up game against a Nicky Oppenheimer XI at his own ground at Randjesfontein. Invitation only. A very upper-class occasion. My first England game since last summer's Edgbaston Test and 1 for 29 in eight overs was a reasonable start.

Wednesday 25th: a day-night game against Eastern Transvaal at Springs. Knock off the 261 with one over to spare thanks to Ramps playing brilliantly. Feel knackered after two one-day games in a row, but get the four-day game off against an Invitation XI in Soweto, which will give my body some breathing space.

Friday 27th: the first first-class game ever played in Soweto. The squad were introduced to Nelson Mandela at lunch. What a great man! He had a small conversation with every player, and everybody felt in awe of him. The respect that people in Soweto showed for him was amazing. Several of the lads are wading through his autobiography.

Monday 30th: the game is abandoned due to rain, and the nets are unusable, too. The ground has been built on an old rubbish tip, hence no drainage system. Meanwhile, Devon has been sent to the nets during the match to try to sort out his action. The Press imagine a feud between Dev and England's bowling coach, Peter Lever.

Tuesday 31st: fly to East London, a windy town on the south coast which reminds me a bit of Brighton. Rooming with JC (John Crawley). The Doc, Philip Bell, has managed to lose his bag, which leaves him without shoes and all our medical records.

President
Mandela meets
the England
players.

NOVEMBER 1995

Thursday 2nd: my first first-class match of the tour against Border. A heavy downpour sends us back to the hotel until play starts at 2 p.m. England batting. In the evening, we are asked to sign the wall in the Sportsman's Bar. A strange request, but it gets us a few complimentary drinks.

Friday 3rd: no play. Played golf in the rain in the afternoon. Others found an amusement arcade and passed the time racing each other on motorbikes. Anything to get out of the hotel.

Saturday 4th: at last! After sixteen days, I bowl my opening first-class over of the tour. It went for five runs that included a nick to third man. I'm nervous, knowing I've got to make an early impression, but I dismiss Franz Cronje – brother of Hansie – with a bouncer which he fends to slip. It's a three-sweater day – as cold as Scarborough in April.

Sunday 5th: we wrapped up Border's first and second innings very easily, and we're very happy with a professional performance.

Monday 6th: early departure to Kimberley, and after a change of planes in Jo'burg, we discover an old mining town with nothing to do. Corky makes his own entertainment by locking Plank (Peter

Lever) out of his room in only a jockstrap. I'm rooming with Peter Martin, who is always pulling funny faces. Bed by 8.30 p.m.

Tuesday 7th: relief, as we finally find some nets with pace and bounce in them. We'll get plenty of that in the Test series. The Press put on a wonderful buffet reception in the evening, but it's a shame their speeches didn't match. At least you can rely on our tour manager, John Barclay, to get the laughter rolling in his wonderful Oxbridge accent. Bed again by 8.30 p.m. – this must be one of the worst places I've toured.

Wednesday 8th: grand opening of 'Yorkshire Cricket Club' (I'm not kidding) at Galeshewe Oval, in a nearby township. I'm in bed for the third successive night by 8.30 p.m., but Digger's snoring wakes me up in the early hours. So I slip on my Spurs shorts and a T-shirt and paddle down to reception to request a single room. They oblige with a slight giggle.

Friday 10th: South Africa A declare on the second day at 450 for 9, and I finish with 3 for 85. Excellent evening as we go shooting with the South African equivalent of the SAS. Teach us how to shoot pistols, shotguns and rifles. Gus (Angus Fraser) had his hat shot to bits before it was returned to him later at the hotel.

Saturday 11th: England follow on. Can't wait to get out of Kimberley.

Sunday 12th: England lose, and Paul Adams, an unorthodox left-arm googly bowler, takes nine wickets in only his second first-class match. No one has seen an action quite like it – he's looking at the floor at the point of delivery. We need a night to cheer us up, but the best we get is Wayne and Ramble on the guitar again!

Monday 13th: fly to Jo'burg, and into a roasting at the team meeting. A fines meeting brings light relief. Raymond (Illingworth) is fined for being the first on tour to get 1,000 runs and 500 wickets. Jack (Russell) collects the Olympic torch award . . . he never goes out.

Tuesday 14th: Illy puts his foot down, replacing our rave music on the bus with Johnny Mathis. That'll teach us to play better. An official welcome dinner in the evening, where South Africa's equivalent to Rory Bremner delivers his whole speech in Afrikaans. Not impressed.

Wednesday 15th: spend the afternoon lying on my bed to inspire Jack on his latest painting . . . an elephant in a game park. He even asks me to sign the back of it by way of thanks. It's the eve of the Test and I'm in the thirteen. Creepy (Crawley), who has started the tour brilliantly, is unlucky to miss out. In the evening we study videos of the South Africans, and I see Schultz and Pollock bowling for the first time.

Thursday 16th: Test match day, and the first thing you notice at breakfast is the quiet. At the ground, Illy and Athers (Michael Atherton) march off the ground to tell me I'm playing, and that Dev and Ramble have missed out. I feel like cheering, but I try to act cool. South Africa put us in, not surprisingly as they're fielding five seamers. Athers is hit on the head three times, and Hicky holds us together with a fine century. *Close, first Test, first day, Centurion Park, Pretoria: England 221 for 4.*

Friday 17th: damn, Corky's out, I'm in. Feel pretty good until the ninth ball. My worst fear – I'm bowled for nought. Afternoon thunderstorm suits my mood. Every dog has his day, and mine will come. *Close, second day: England 381 for 9.*

Saturday 18th: rain forces a 2 p.m. call-off. I send a card and a toy tractor back home for Liam's birthday. Goodbyes to our batting and bowling coaches – Messrs Edrich and Lever. The physio pens them a poem as a send-off. *Close, third day: England 381 for 9.*

Sunday 19th: still raining. Bored, so play picture charades. Very bored, so play hangman. While treating our security guard for a bad hamstring, Wayne whitens his legs with shoe whitener. That sort of day. *Close, fourth day: England 381 for 9.*

Monday 20th: weather brightens up for a while, so it's on with the suntan lotion and the zinc cream. The ten-minute bell goes, and then another downpour begins. Match abandoned. We'd have won it on points, but we badly need some bowling. *Final scores: England 381 for 9. Match drawn.*

Tuesday 21st: the team song on this tour is 'Oh Sit Down', by James, and we give a rendition while boarding the plane, en route to Bloemfontein. Arrive at the hotel to Zulu dancers.

Wednesday 22nd: nets unfit. Golf course unfit. Time for sprints.

Thursday 23rd: first day of a three-day match against Orange Free State and, after Athers goes for nought, Stewart and Thorpe cash in on a good batting strip with hundreds. I'm not playing. Ring home to discover that Liam has taken his first steps. Watch the Princess Diana interview after dinner – some of her answers are amazing, but I have to admire her courage.

Friday 24th: forget my twelfth man duties at a drinks break. Didn't go down too well.

Saturday 25th: after yesterday's slip-up, drinks in mid-afternoon gives me a chance to get my own back. I pile two bar stools, a television, CD player, fruit, chocolate and every conceivable drink on to the golf cart. The lads respond by nicking the keys, so I have to push it part way back to the pavilion. The game was heading for a boring draw, so it cheered everyone up.

Sunday 26th: one-day game against Orange Free State, and we slaughter them on a turning wicket.

Monday 27th: early flight back to our second home – the Sandton Sun, Jo'burg. Rory, the VIP policeman whose legs were whitened by Wayne last week, gets his own back by arranging for the physio to be arrested at the airport on drugs charges. They even fingerprinted him before bringing him back to the hotel where we were waiting to clap him in. Very funny.

Special delivery for the lads at a drinks interval in Bloemfontein.

Tuesday 28th: practise half an hour away at Centurion Park, because we think the facilities are better than at the Wanderers. At the nets, my favourite bat snaps in half.

Wednesday 29th: raining again. Surely another Test can't be washed out. Have a chat with Freddie Trueman, who agrees to watch me during the Test if I'm selected.

Thursday 30th: get the nod at 9.30 a.m. England play four seamers and leave out Ilott and Illingworth. But I bowl poorly in the morning session and Gary Kirsten goes on to register his first Test hundred. Bon Jovi concert in the evening. I'm not a big fan, but we talk our way into the VIP room afterwards. I need cheering up. *Close, second Test, first day, Wanderers, Johannesburg: South Africa 278 for 7.*

DECEMBER 1995

Friday 1st: spend a fearful couple of hours in a Johannesburg hospital, awaiting an X-ray on my arm. I was struck by Brian McMillan while batting, and I'm scared that for the second successive year my tour might be about to end early. Fortunately, the X-ray reveals only bad bruising and I live to fight another day. We batted badly today against a straight and aggressive South African attack. I spend the evening icing my arm and praying that I'll be able to bowl tomorrow. *Close, second day: South Africa 332 and 5 for 0; England 200.*

Saturday 2nd: we walk on to the field to the strains of 'Land of Hope and Glory' and 'God Save The Queen'. The Jo'burg crowd stands in appreciation. My arm is heavily strapped and I write across it: 'No pain, no gain. Be strong.' But still the force was not with us. With two days remaining, South Africa are in a commanding position. *Close, third day: South Africa 332 and 296 for 6; England 200.*

Sunday 3rd: South Africa declare nine down, setting us 470 to win or, more realistically, five and a quarter sessions to save the game. We finish the day four wickets down. Jack Russell's eleven catches beat Bob Taylor's world record and Bob is one of the first to congratulate him as he leaves the field. We throw a champagne reception for Jack back at the hotel. He says he's very honoured, but that his biggest thrill would be to save the

Test. *Close, fourth day: South Africa 332 and 346 for 9 declared; England 200 and 167 for 4.*

Monday 4th: the Barmy Army is in full swing again and up on the players' balcony we're in the mood to party with them. Against all the odds, we've saved the Test. Michael Atherton plays an awesome innings, batting for nearly eleven hours in making 185 not out, an innings of monumental determination. It's the fourth-longest Test innings in England history and no one can ever have shown more clearly what it should mean to play for his country. Jack's wish is granted, too, as he faces 235 balls for his unbeaten 29. This has been my worst England Test. I haven't taken a wicket and I've been hit by big Brian McMillan to boot. But this has cheered me up no end. *Final scores: South Africa 332 and 346 for 9 declared; England 200 and 351 for 5. Match drawn.*

Tuesday 5th: bags outside by 6.30 a.m., and another early flight as we raid the departure lounge of crisps, bread rolls and biscuits. These early departures certainly encourage bad eating habits. A bus from Cape Town takes us to Paarl, another quiet town. Excellent evening barbecue at a local vineyard.

Wednesday 6th: after nets, run back to the hotel to burn off some of the frustration of the last Test. In the afternoon, Paul Nixon, the Leicestershire 'keeper, drives Corky, Ramps and myself on the forty-five-minute journey into Cape Town in his clapped-out Golf. We're visiting Daffy (Phil DeFreitas), who is wintering in a lovely flat overlooking the sea.

Thursday 7th: the South Africans have certainly done their planning. In between Tests, we are playing on slow wickets which give us no chance of good preparation. Fail with the bat, dragging the ball on, but my luck must change soon.

Friday 8th: yet another niggle – this time at the back of the knee/hamstring.

Saturday 9th: my hundredth first-class match has been a nightmare. I fail a fitness test this morning, and it looks as though I'm out of the third Test. The Boland game is so boring that we abandon it and have a one-day match instead. We haven't had a good game yet in five first-class matches.

Thursday 14th: my hamstring injury will put me out of the

Durban Test. It's been hard to swallow. After this match there are back-to-back Tests over Christmas and New Year, with no chance in between for fringe players to press their claims. Once a tour starts going wrong, it can be difficult to pull it back. You just have to keep working hard and hope for a lucky break. *Close, third Test, first day, Kingsmead, Durban: South Africa 139 for 5.*

Friday 15th: one hour's fielding and John Crawley becomes our first real casualty of the tour. He tears a hamstring while chasing a ball to the boundary and will definitely miss the rest of the Test series. He might have to put some pads on in our first innings though – we are struggling after losing five cheap wickets. It's shocking luck for JC after all the fitness work he has put in since returning from Australia. Jason Gallian is summoned as a replacement from the A tour in Pakistan. Finding a direct route from Peshawar to Durban defeats the travel agents. The lads reckon he might be here by Christmas! *Close, second day: South Africa 225; England 123 for 5.*

Saturday 16th: farmers are advised to move their cattle to high ground. The rain is bucketing down. *Close, third day: South Africa 225; England 152 for 5.*

Sunday 17th: it rains all day, so Sky TV show some footage which tries to suggest that South Africa's seamer, Craig Matthews, has been ball-tampering. Suppose they have to get something for their money. Pass the time watching the latest James Bond movie, *Goldeneye,* and at a sports forum for Kuoni Travel's supporters, where Angus (Fraser) and I enjoy answering questions about what cricket was like twenty-five years ago. Illy's not there to give an alternative view. *Close, fourth day: South Africa 225; England 152 for 5.*

Monday 18th: game cancelled as soon as we arrive at the ground. Tourists planning to drive into Kwa Zulu-Natal are warned to watch out for floods and mud slides. What sort of weather is this? We dream of rain this heavy when we're exhausted in the middle of an English season. *Final scores: South Africa 225; England 152 for 5. Match drawn.*

Wednesday 20th: team bus breaks down on the motorway on the way to Pietermaritzburg to play the South African students. The Fizz (the physio, Wayne Morton) nearly fixes that as well. Is there anything he can't do? Wives, girlfriends and children arrive midday and the five of us not playing are allowed to leave early. I can hardly believe that the boy standing up in my hotel room with all that hair is actually Liam. It takes him ten minutes to realise who I am and, to top the day, he walks more than two steps for the first time. After nine weeks, it's great to see the family again. Even Mum and Dad are here. My aim is to play in the final Test in Cape Town so they can see me play for England overseas.

Sunday 24th: even Father Christmas has to change his schedule when there's a Test match to play. Our very own Father Christmas (scorer Malcolm Ashton) gives out the presents at the kiddies' party in Port Elizabeth on Christmas Eve. Then once we've packed them all off to bed, it's time for karaoke for the players and their better halves. Vandana Ramprakash and I are paired to sing 'The Locomotion', while Anna teams up with Robin Smith in a hilarious rendition of 'The Lion Sleeps Tonight'.

Monday 25th: Christmas Day begins with a two-hour net session. We've suspended our traditional lunchtime fancy dress party this year in favour of a barbecue around the pool. The hotel catering is not helped when two chefs walk out, taking most of the staff with them.

Tuesday 26th: good toss to win – and South Africa win it. Looks like we're on the back foot again. *Close, fourth Test, first day, St George's Park, Port Elizabeth: South Africa 231 for 4.*

Wednesday 27th: the South Africans bat most of the day. Ramble (Mark Ilott) tears his thigh, which is bad luck both for him and the team. I wouldn't be human, though, if I didn't wonder about my chances now of playing in the final Test in Cape Town. *Close, second day: South Africa 428; England 40 for 1.*

Thursday 28th: Test matches can swing on a single moment, and we're hoping that Michael Atherton's dismissal today is not one of them. Athers does well to keep his cool, but there is no disguising his distress as he is given out caught down the legside off the googly and chinaman bowler, Paul Adams. At least we've avoided the follow-on. *Close, third day: South Africa 428; England 250 for 7.*

Friday 29th: Dermot Reeve OBE has joined us for the one-day series and probably the World Cup to follow. Naturally, we're all craving an audience. If he helps us win the World Cup, he'll probably be knighted. The Test livens up with Corky's five wickets giving us a glimpse of victory. *Close, fourth day: South Africa 428 and 162 for 9 dec.; England 263 and 20 for 0.*

Saturday 30th: the St George's Road brass band keep going until the end, but the Test gradually dies away on a deathly slow pitch. It's another stalemate, but even that can demand a lot of dedication and hard work. Alec Stewart buckles down to the job for five and a half hours in making 81. *Final scores: South Africa 428 and 162 for 9 dec.; England 263 and 189 for 3. Match drawn.*

JANUARY 1995

Monday 1st: last night was a New Year's Eve party at the British Consulate and, after the year I've had, nobody raised their glass higher to 1996. But the year has begun badly. Although I'm fit again, I'm out of the team for the final Test.

Tuesday 2nd: the final showdown begins very much in South Africa's favour. Without the Judge (Robin Smith), we would have been in even worse trouble. *Close, fifth Test, first day, Newlands, Cape Town: England 153; South Africa 44 for 2.*

Wednesday 3rd: three months of hard work are threatened by an unbelievable final hour. When South Africa's ninth wicket falls, they are only 19 ahead, and our bowlers have toughed it out magnificently. With the chance to bowl last on a newly laid strip, we must be favourites. Then South Africa's last pair, Allan Donald and Paul Adams, add 73, an enormous blow in a low-scoring game. *Close, second day: England 153 and 17 for 1; South Africa 244.*

Thursday 4th: disaster as South Africa take the series. We've been convinced all along that we are the better side, but all we've earned is another England Test series defeat overseas. The depression is aggravated as half the party go down with food poisoning – probably the lunchtime pasta. But there's no time to be morbid – the World Cup is on the horizon. *Final scores: England 153 and 157; South Africa 244 and 70 for 0. South Africa win by 10 wickets, and take Test series 1–0.*

4   Red, White and Blue

The severe pain shooting through my left foot immediately told me that my Ashes adventure was over. As I was chair-lifted from the Melbourne Cricket Ground by Shaun Udal and Dave Roberts, the England physio, I became aware of an ovation from 73,000 spectators. And that was when I began to cry.

For nearly three months on my first overseas tour, I'd had the time of my life. I'd relished the Australian way of life, and the Australian public seemed to have taken me to their hearts. They were not used to Englishmen being so brash and belligerent. Everything I touched had seemed to turn to gold. Earlier that evening, while batting, I had teased the Australian bowlers with a reverse sweep and a flick to leg from outside off stump. One English journalist wrote that I must sit up at night thinking of new gags.

Then, as I jumped into the crease to deliver the first ball in Australia's innings, everything turned sour. Instead of looking forward to two more Test matches, and the razzmatazz of the Benson & Hedges World Series finals, it was time to think of lonely airport lounges, and a heartbreaking reunion with my family in a chilly English winter. They had been on their way out to see me, and had to be turned back at the last minute.

There are some critics, perhaps, who still suspect that I will never recover the success I enjoyed that winter, that the acclaim that sounded for my refreshing entrance into the England side will never be as loud again. They reckon, simply, that I'll prove to be a flash in the pan. Well, one thing's for sure. I'm not going to rest until I've proved them wrong.

When I was invalided out of the Ashes series, I had twenty wickets in three Tests – only one fewer than Shane Warne and Craig McDermott had at the same stage for Australia, and they had caused havoc. I reckon that is a record to take heart from. The third Test in Sydney, over New Year, still ranks as the greatest match of my life. We badly needed a boost after a 295-run defeat in the Christmas Test in Melbourne had caused criticism to rain upon us. Fourteen defeats and only one win in the last twenty-one

My Australia tour is over as I'm helped from the field in agony.

Tests against Australia told its own story and newspaper columns were bursting with proposed remedies for the English game..

Warne had become Australia's national hero. He had finished us off in Melbourne with a hat-trick – I have to admit that I was the middle man in it – and the mickey-taking was coming thick and fast. One Aussie wanted to know if 'all you Poms pad up at once'. There was no point moping, we had to hit back adventurously.

When I went out to bat in Sydney, I told the lads to 'fasten their seat belts'. Keith Fletcher, the England coach, had encouraged me to play my natural game, and it worked a treat as I got

50 in no time, including a few swashbuckling shots against McDermott.

But the real treat was to follow that up with 6 for 49 in Australia's first innings as we bowled them out for 116. I managed to dismiss Australia's captain, Mark Taylor, with a leg break and, by my own calculations, bowled pretty fast and accurately. The English Press, desperate for some good news, went to town. But my lucky bracelet was on its last threads. Perhaps I should have regarded that as an omen . . . a week later I was heading for hospital.

An Ashes tour must rank as one of the greatest joys in sport. I'm a proud Englishman, and always will be, but Australia's free-and-easy outdoor life filled me with delight. Yorkshiremen and Australians both have a habit of saying what they think – sometimes even putting their mouth into gear before engaging brain. It seems to me that it all makes for a more straightforward life.

Things had gone well from the word go. The presence of four all-time Australian greats – Dennis Lillee, Jeff Thomson, Greg Chappell and Rod Marsh – in the tour's pipe-opener at Lilac Hill, just outside Perth, meant that I was aching to create a good impression. We gave them a lift to the ground in the team coach and there was some playful banter about it turning into a time machine.

Five wickets did me no harm at all, including Greg Chappell, and I won't tell anyone in future that he was forty-six years old! Lillee made some favourable comments about me after the match. Hearing one of your childhood heroes praising you can give you the shivers.

There was a month's build-up before the first Test in Brisbane, which left the tabloids plenty of scope for unusual stories. One of their most imaginative efforts was to suggest that I'd been close to drowning when surfing at Newcastle Bar Beach. It was exhausting, but I'm quite a strong swimmer and I never felt in danger and it was quite a surprise to see a lifeguard swimming towards me.

Another great honour was to meet one of England's greatest-ever fast bowlers, Harold Larwood, at his bungalow just three miles from Sydney Cricket Ground. 'Lol' had lived forty-four of his ninety years in Australia, but he was still a Pom at heart. I asked him if he had ever pitched the ball up when bowling to his Bodyline field of four short legs. 'Did I what?' he exclaimed. 'Never!'

Surfing with Phil Tufnell on the beach at Newcastle. And what is more, I'm still alive to tell the tale ...

It was with considerable sadness that I heard of Larwood's death last summer. I'll never forget that he encouraged me to recover the Ashes for England, and told me that there was no better feeling in the world. We couldn't do it for him on this occasion – eventually losing the series 3–1 – but I hope one day to discover if he is right.

The first day of the Brisbane Test ranks as one of the happiest of my life. Hours before my Ashes debut, I received a phone call from Anna at 7.30 a.m. to tell me that she'd given birth to Liam, our first child. It was three days later before I caught a glimpse of him, downloaded on to the computer of Graham Morris, one of the regular 'snappers' on England tours.

The rumour that Liam's middle names would be the names of any Aussie batsman I dismissed was soon being whispered round the Press box. It wasn't true, but I did dismiss David Boon and Michael Bevan by the close, and finished with six wickets in the match. Not that there was much for England to celebrate – Australia won by 184 runs as Warne had a field day, taking eight wickets in the second innings. He was to haunt us all tour.

It had been a rollercoaster eight months as an England player. I'd toured South Africa with the A squad the previous winter and sensed that I'd done enough to put myself in contention for a Test spot. It had taken me a long time on the A tour to grab the limelight, but I finished very much on a high, taking twenty-three first-class wickets at 25 each and finishing with seven wickets in the unofficial Test in Port Elizabeth. Most importantly, I began to reverse swing the old ball, and caused a few eyebrows to raise as a result – not least my own. It was a priceless discovery as most of the pitches were slow and lacking in bounce, so you just had to buckle down to the job.

As far as the one-day squad was concerned, I thought I had no chance, so I was speechless on 15 May, 1994, to find myself in the Texaco Trophy squad against New Zealand. Raymond Illingworth, the new chairman of selectors, had made an immediate impression, keeping only seven of the tourists in the Caribbean that winter. Illy praised my improvement, saying, 'He became fitter, quicker and more controlled.'

Athers was to judge a few days later, 'After Devon Malcolm, he's as quick as anyone in the country. He has a good yorker, a good slower ball, a good attitude and good prospects.'

There were some who thought I was lucky to be included ahead of Somerset's Andrew Caddick, but I was on a high, and celebrated with 4 for 20 – my best Sunday League figures – against Glamorgan at Cardiff.

The five days until the first one-dayer at Old Trafford were probably the longest of my life. I couldn't go more than a couple of minutes without looking ahead to my England debut. It was vital to make an immediate impression, because Athers had said that I'd probably only play one game of the two. And what a start I was to have – the wicket of Martin Crowe, one of the top batsmen in the world, with my sixth ball.

My first wicket for England will always be one of my favourites. I had begun right on song, making Crowe hop around a bit. My sixth ball seemed to startle him for pace as his attempted cut was clutched high above his head by Alec Stewart at first slip.

But the ball that received most plaudits came in my second spell as I produced an inswinging yorker to remove Bryan Young, whose 65 had held New Zealand's innings together. Illy commented that I seemed able to call on the inswinging yorker as much as Wasim or Waqar which, not surprisingly, caused the Press boys to prick their ears up. 'My Waqar' was how I was billed in one headline the next day! There I was, after one day's international cricket, touted as England's answer to not just one, but two, of the finest fast bowlers in the world. It all seemed like fantasy land.

An ache in my side made sure that I didn't get carried away.

Martin Crowe departs, caught at the wicket, and I have my first wicket for England.

As the excitement died away, I became increasingly aware that I had not got through my first international injury-free. There was no prospect of playing in the rest of the one-day series and, in fact, it was late June before I returned for Yorkshire against Hampshire at Headingley. After a tough workout – more than fifty overs in the match – I was named for the third Cornhill Test against New Zealand at Old Trafford. Two more intense net sessions helped to convince both the selectors and myself that I was a hundred per cent fit.

All I wanted to do was to pull on the sweater with the three lions and bowl for my country. Old Trafford was one of my favourite wickets in the country, one where Peter Marron, the head groundsman, had succeeded in introducing a little more pace and bounce. Nerves were also not a problem. Sure, I had a few butterflies before the game – there is something wrong if you don't – but as far as I was concerned, the bigger the occasion, the better. My Texaco debut had caused a lot of expectancy, but there was no point worrying about that. I couldn't wait for the game to start.

Thanks to Steve Rhodes, who had staved off defeat with a gritty last-session innings at Lord's, we went into the final Test one-up, and we were determined not to toss away the advantage. But we did not begin the second day well, collapsing to 235 for 7, before I enjoyed another day that I'll not forget in a hurry.

I've always fancied myself as a bit of an adventurer as a batsman – I know I can bat, it's just that I keep doing something daft – but even I had never assumed that that was how I would make my first big impression.

I'd immediately struck up a rapport off the field with Phil DeFreitas and we conjured up a stand of 130 for the eighth wicket to steer us away from trouble. Mike Selvey, in the *Guardian*, reckoned I looked like a young farmer enjoying himself at a county fair. What was certain was that Daffy and I enjoyed ourselves. If you do that, it can clear a lot of complications from your mind.

Every time one of us played an attacking shot, the other tried to cap it with something even more outrageous. But I lost a little momentum after Daffy got out and soon afterwards, on 65, chipped Chris Pringle to cover. Both of us lamented in the dressing room the maiden Test centuries that had got away.

That optimism flooded into my bowling later in the day as I took a wicket with my first over in Test cricket. Mark Greatbatch was opening the New Zealand innings with a broken thumb, which gave me a great opportunity to work him over early. He had struggled against short-pitched balls all summer and my fifth legitimate delivery – the third was a no-ball – did the trick as he fended a delivery hurtling into his ribcage to Graeme Hick at second slip.

The Saturday became a Yorkshire sideshow. I blasted out Matthew Hart with my first ball of the day, Chalkie White bowled quickly to take three wickets, including Crowe, and when I added the wicket of Michael Owens, New Zealand were forced to follow on. By Saturday's close, with New Zealand 205 for 5, still 26 runs behind, we sensed we were well on our way to a 2–0 series victory. In the end, a combination of Crowe, with an accomplished century, and appalling Manchester weather for most of the last two days, meant that we had to settle for 1– 0.

It was just over a year since I had trailed away from Edgbaston, after a Yorkshire championship match, knowing that I was heading back to the 2nd XI and wondering whether I had any future in the game. It was then that I realised I had to give it my all. It was remarkable how quickly things had changed.

Sunday was a rest day and, while most of the England lads went to a barbecue thrown by the physio, Dave Roberts, I headed back over the Pennines to spend some time with the family and try to let it all sink in. Jack, my Jack Russell terrier, greeted me as warmly as ever and I took him off for a walk wondering if it had all really happened. Suddenly, a place on the winter tour to Australia looked a real possibility.

South Africa were next in line for a three-Test series and Mike Procter, their coach, had made some comments about England being a soft touch. We were determined to prove him wrong.

The Lord's Test will always be remembered for the 'ball-tampering' allegations levelled against Michael Atherton – a story which came to be known as 'the dirt in the pocket affair'. To crash to a 356-run defeat against South Africa, and fear that we might lose an inspirational young captain in the process, was dispiriting for every England player. The last thing I wanted was for Athers to be forced to resign amid an atmosphere of innuendo and ignorance just as my own future was looking so rosy.

Athers' insistence that he was not cheating will do for me, and that's all I'm going to say on the matter, apart from one final point. Reverse swing is a relatively new art, especially outside India and Pakistan, which has caused a good deal of confusion. But, at my best, I can reverse swing the ball, and I do it legally. Ball-tampering might quicken the process, but don't assume that every time the ball reverses somebody has been cheating. That couldn't be further from the truth.

Headingley was next up – my first home Test, with the hopes of the Yorkshire public riding on me. I remember wearing a Fred Trueman 'Legends' T-shirt, but I was certainly not chasing any comparisons with Fred, Ian Botham or Uncle Tom Cobbley. I just wanted to be accepted as Darren Gough, a boisterous lad, blessed with a bit of talent, trying to make his way in the game.

The Western Terrace was in full voice. It had been thirteen

years since the last Yorkshireman, Chris Old, had played in a Test at Headingley, and now three of us – myself, Steve Rhodes and Craig White – were all in the side. The ovation I received when I walked to the wicket made me wonder if the crowd knew something I didn't! When Rhodesy and myself put together a half-century stand during England's first-innings score of 477, every run was cheered to the rooftops. Or at least it would have been if the Western Terrace, one of the Test grounds' more primitive stands, had as much as a roof. Then to cap the day, I had Andrew Hudson caught at slip. The adrenalin never stopped pumping all day.

The innings of real character, though, had been played by Athers, whose response to what must have been the worst ten days of his life was to grind out an innings of 99. Headingley turned out to be very much a batsman's match. After the excitement of the second day, I bowled one of my worst England spells on Saturday and finished with 2 for 153, South Africa's 443 ensuring a draw.

England's eight-wicket win at The Oval, to level the series, and so complete a satisfactory summer, will always be known as Devon Malcolm's match. Dev's 9 for 57 was raw fast bowling at its best, unmatched by an Englishman since Jim Laker spun out the Aussies in 1956. He might have even taken all ten had I not managed to nip out Darryl Cullinan, whose 94 had proved that he, more than anyone, had the stomach for a fight.

I was happy for someone else to grab the attention, especially such a warmhearted character as Dev. But Illy could not resist putting in another good word for me, praising another lower-order adventurous stand between myself and Daffy in England's first innings – 59 runs in an exhilarating last half-hour of play – for getting us on our way. Less than a fortnight later, my place on the Ashes tour was confirmed..

Since my return from Australia with a double fracture of my foot, things have not gone too well for me. Last summer was always going to demand a good deal of rehabilitation, but several injury niggles made it more frustrating than ever. Most judges reckoned that our 2–2 draw against the West Indies reflected our steady improvement, but I couldn't claim to have played much of a part in it. Once again, Headingley proved to be a disappointment. Giving the Yorkshire supporters a Test to remember has become one of my greatest ambitions. I'll be busting a gut to ensure that they don't have to wait too long.

5 Born and Bred

Eee lad, me Lord's debut fer Yorkshire left me fair gobsmacked. Ah were so nervous ah were jiggered before ah started. For a gormless lad used to neea coils int' skep and an outside privy, it were enough to mek me pittle me britches.

That tongue-in-cheek version of my first game for Yorkshire is dedicated to the cricket writer who delighted in miscasting me on my first-class debut against Middlesex as the 'son of a Barnsley rat catcher'. My dad was nothing of the sort. He was a service technician for Rentokil, and had hardly seen a rat in his life, but I could certainly smell one.

I'm proud of being born and bred in Yorkshire, but didn't expect to be stereotyped quite so quickly. I've never believed in being too precious about the media, but I can't say I was too happy about my first brush with it. It was sheer prejudice. My team-mates soon made sure I buckled down again, particularly our skipper, David Bairstow, who stomped around doing his Mr Angry routine. Not that it stopped him nicknaming me Roland, after the breakfast TV rat puppet!

I had realised that a Yorkshire debut was in the offing when Phil Carrick, Yorkshire's captain, asked me if I had ever been to London. I had to admit that I hadn't. As an eighteen-year-old lad, I still had much to learn.

If going to London on the train was a totally new experience, merely finding my way around Lord's was exhausting. I didn't quite finish up in the gents' like David Steele when he was going out to bat for England against Australia in 1975, but it was a close-run thing. And then I read that my dad was supposed to be a 'ratty.' Charles Randall, of the *Daily Telegraph*, was not about to join my Christmas card list in a hurry.

It quickly underlined that Yorkshire will always be different. I live in a proud county, often opinionated, sometimes slow to change, but determined, warm-hearted and immensely loyal. Nothing has done more to nurture the county's self-esteem over the last hundred years than the strength of Yorkshire cricket.

But when I made my debut in 1989, pessimism abounded over some of the leanest times in the club's history.

Yorkshire have made important strides since then, strides which I am convinced are already heralding a new era. The outdated reliance solely upon on players born within the county boundaries was abandoned in 1990, and rightly so in an age of such mobility. In the time it used to take to journey the length of Yorkshire, you can now travel around the world.

Nor was there any justification in Yorkshire handicapping its own players by refusing to sanction the signing of an overseas player. When that tradition was abandoned in 1991, I was as thrilled as anybody. Life had been dispiriting as we faced overseas fast bowlers on sharp pitches without any chance to fight fire with fire. Times had changed, and Yorkshire had to be allowed to compete on equal terms. Indeed, had the West Indies captain, Richie Richardson, never played for Yorkshire, I might never have been given the advice that made me an England bowler. What possible good would that have done for Yorkshire or for me?

When things are going badly, it is far too easy to stick your head in the sands. Perhaps Yorkshire have been more guilty of that in the past than most.

As a far more worthwhile proof of its commitment to its young players, the Park Avenue Yorkshire Cricket Academy is now producing a steady stream of talent: Michael Vaughan, Anthony McGrath and Alex Morris are just a few of the names that are going to mean an awful lot in the future. Yorkshire cannot keep every youngster it produces, but as long as those in charge have the nous to pick the best, then the future is brighter than it has been for a generation. My future is committed to Yorkshire and I'm desperate to play in a championship-winning side before I retire.

One thing we do need to sort out at Yorkshire is our pitches. Most counties deliberately prepare pitches to suit their strengths, but the groundsmen for Yorkshire's home matches can be an awkward, unpredictable lot.

Keith Boyce's last track at Headingley before he retired as groundsman at the end of last season to concentrate on his Rugby League duties was for a championship match against Middlesex. We still had a chance of finishing in the top four and as Middlesex were lacking their three top seamers – Angus Fraser, Dion Nash and Richard Johnson – and were heavily reliant upon their two spinners – Phil Tufnell and John Emburey – we were looking forward to a typical Headingley seamer. Astonishingly, Boycey prepared the first Headingley turner that anyone could remember. Boycey's pitches had been getting better and better, but this was a curious 'goodbye'. Sure enough, Embers and Tuffers spun us out twice. As far as pace bowling was concerned, we might as well have played a couple of YTS lads and given everyone else four days off.

I'd always been more interested in football as a kid, although I was fortunate that at Priory School they made the best of their limited facilities and always encouraged both. I played for Barnsley Schools from under-11s upwards, and I was a YTS trialist at Rotherham United for three months. There was no choice but to wander down to the Job Centre when that fell by the wayside, and fortunately my sporting ability bailed me out again when I joined the Headingley indoor cricket school – a joint venture between Yorkshire and Leeds City Council – as a YTS lad. Before long I was attached to the Yorkshire Cricket Academy at Park Avenue. My old mate Paul Grayson, now with Essex, was another Yorkshire player to travel the same route.

Steve Oldham took me under his wing. In those days, 'Esso' largely coached the youngsters and was regarded as the font of all wisdom, a voice of authority. I hadn't played too many games for Yorkshire Schools – coming from Barnsley, you don't always have the 'right connections' – but Esso held me in higher regard. It was not long before I moved from my village club, Monk Bretton, to Barnsley in the Yorkshire League. Monk Bretton waved me off with good wishes, just as they had with another Yorkshire and England player, Martyn Moxon, a few years earlier. All small clubs must be willing to develop their young players, not desperately cling on to them, if English club cricket is ever going to do itself justice.

I had first caught Yorkshire's attention during a testimonial match for Arnie Sidebottom the previous season when I took 4 for 11 on my Barnsley debut, dismissing Moxon, Bairstow, Phil Carrick and Phil Robinson. But, if truth were told, in April 1989, after the release of Simon Dennis, and with injuries to Chris Shaw, Stuart Fletcher and Peter Hartley, I was about the only bowler left.

Even I had doubts about a sore back, but I wouldn't have admitted to that under hypnosis. Middlesex at Lord's was my big chance, and it could not have gone better as I took 5 for 91 in the match and Mike Gatting presented me with an engraved tankard as the first YTS trainee to represent the county. Afterwards I caused a few raised eyebrows by saying that I enjoyed walking out to bat best. Arnie Sidebottom wasn't too impressed, though. He saw me face a couple of balls at number eleven from Angus Fraser and Neil Williams, and then got himself out, having a slog. 'I want to see you stay alive,' he said.

Paul Downton was my first victim, caught at slip by Arnie, but it was Gatt's dismissal in the second innings that left me bursting with pride. Gatt edged my first ball past Paul Jarvis at catchable height at second slip, but Jarv didn't flex a muscle. Then he nicked my second ball through the slips for four. The third was nothing special, but he turned it to Dick Blakey at midwicket. The next thing I knew, Bairstow was squeezing the life from me with an exuberant bear-hug.

That was virtually the end of my season. I was in so much discomfort that I had an X-ray, and discovered that I was suffering from a stress fracture. Bowling thirteen successive overs in the second innings had not done me any favours, especially since my body was not in the best of shape in those days. Yorkshire were in desperate straits that year. Apart from Sidebottom and Carrick, both approaching the end of their careers, Jarv was the only other bowler to average under 40 in first-class cricket. When Carrick wrote an open letter to the Yorkshire committee, demanding that the Yorkshire-only policy be abandoned, the support in the dressing room was as good as unanimous.

Despite the disruption caused by my back injury, the first season had whetted my appetite. I could still dream about the chance of becoming a regular in the Yorkshire side. But the next two seasons were the most dismal of my career. As the Yorkshire committee continued to squabble over the rights and wrongs of employing an overseas player, Moxon and Oldham (a new captain and coach) struggled to shake off an air of pessimism. We tried to play positively but, in the days of three-day cricket, we had little chance of bowling a side out twice. Most of our efforts went into trying to fiddle a last-afternoon run-chase.

Once depression takes hold of a side, it is remarkably difficult to shift. Because we had no strike weapon, we were constantly on the back foot. Because of the weakness of our bowling, our batsmen often had to bat on sub-standard pitches, produced by opponents confident of a quick killing.

Sidebottom was approaching the end of his career, and needed two knee operations; Fletcher wasn't retained; Jarvis, our classiest bowler, was dropped. Everywhere you looked, the picture was bleak. There was hardly anybody to turn to for advice. Most of those who were fit were so worried about their own careers that they were either unwilling or unable to offer any help at all. It would have been one heck of a budding fast bowler, in 1990, who could have turned that to his advantage.

I didn't. In fact, I didn't enjoy my cricket at all. I was sick of losing, sick of the certainty that this Yorkshire side could not satisfy the high demands of its public. If someone had offered me a job outside cricket, for about £25,000 a year, I would have jumped at it. I'd simply had enough.

Peter Hartley was the one player to offer some advice, and to lift my spirits. PJ probably wishes that he had taken up golf, not cricket, and he can give the impression that he would rather put his feet up and watch the TV in the dressing room than play another day's cricket, but once on the field, he never gives in. That's why his career has lasted deep into his thirties. It is not what you say, but what you do that counts.

I was delighted that Pete had the season of his life in 1995. Most people will remember it as the second dryest summer since records began, but Pete will look with most pleasure upon a cool and damp May and June, when the pitches were seaming and he cashed in like no one else in the land. His opportunity to lead the Yorkshire attack had come late in life, but he took it. A new ball, a choice of ends, a chance to bowl at the tail, the opportunity to bowl when you want to – they can all contribute to a senior bowler's success rate. To those who dismiss PJ as a journeyman, I say that I recall the day at Sophia Gardens when he spun Viv Richards' cap around his head. He was unlucky that I nipped in to bowl him before he could follow it up!

On 10 July, 1991, Yorkshire's general committee announced their intention to employ an overseas player; nine days later, they announced the signing of the Aussie fast bowler, Craig McDermott, for the following season. Remarkably quick work, and I must have been impressed, because *Wisden* records that I finished the season with 'something of a flourish'.

For much of the season I had been limited to twelfth-man

duties (except on the flat decks when I generally played!), which taught me little other than how to brew tea and read road maps. At twenty-one, and single, I rarely needed a second invitation to go out for the night, have a few drinks, and forget my troubles.

But the Roses match at Scarborough was the climax to the season that I needed: an unbeaten 60 in Yorkshire's first innings of 501 for 6 declared and then my first five-wicket haul – 5 for 41 – to bowl us to victory in the second innings. Without that win, we could easily have finished bottom of the championship.

The match ended in extraordinary fashion with Ian Austin laying into Carrick's slow left arm so savagely that he reached his century in 61 balls, the fastest of the season. That just proved how quickly a Yorkshire crowd could turn – 'Good old Fergie' became 'You useless fat lump' in a matter of minutes.

My visions of pumping McDermott for everything he knew about fast bowling were soon abandoned as he pulled out of his contract, stating the need for a groin operation. Instead, Yorkshire's first overseas player became the Indian, Sachin Tendulkar, who was hugely popular with players and public alike, and helped to remove the misconceptions that Yorkshire's homegrown policy had been racistly motivated. It was not too long before he was asked to pose for pictures in Yorkshire flat cap, brandishing a pint of Tetley bitter.

Sachin was clearly a teenage prodigy. He upstaged us from the moment he flew in, turning up at The Oval in rugby shirt, jeans and trainers – a far cry from Yorkshire's stuffy insistence upon blazer and tie. Nobody said a word. He had looked a wonderkid on the TV, but only when I actually bowl at someone do I form a definite opinion about how good they are. One net session against Sachin was enough to convince me that he was a genius.

In truth, though, Sachin was not quite what we needed. Aside from the preference for a fast bowler, he was too young to educate a dressing room desperate for a lead. We needed a leg-up, someone inspirational, able to impart the knowledge gleaned from years of experience. If Sachin came back to Yorkshire now, he would probably be perfect. Then, it was just too early. He managed his 1,000 championship runs and his only hundred helped us to beat Durham. But after all the ballyhoo, sixteenth was another disappointing finish, and my own improvements were masked by inaccuracy. Clearly, there was going to be no easy fix.

I would be lying if I said that I hadn't also noticed that my old mate, Dominic Cork, had slipped into the England Texaco Trophy side against Pakistan. Corky and I had played in the same England under-19 side, and we had always enjoyed a few beers together whenever Yorkshire and Derbyshire came into opposition. His success made me realise that I had to start sifting carefully through the advice I was getting. There was no danger of me becoming any quieter in the dressing room, though.

In May 1993, my dad, Trevor, was still keeping cuttings of my seven-wicket performance for Shepley in the Huddersfield League. By September, I was chosen for the England A tour to South Africa. A year later, I made my England one-day debut. That is how quickly fortunes can change. And the man that had so much to do with it was the West Indies captain, Richie Richardson.

Richie's one and a half seasons at Yorkshire were deeply troubled. The demanding international treadmill was beginning to take its toll on one of the most genial cricketers in the game. He was always close to fatigue and it was no surprise when he eventually left us midway during the summer of '94 because of nervous exhaustion. His personal life was also full of anguish. During his first year with us, his mother died, and the next summer his son was injured in a road accident back in Antigua. Ari was occasionally seen practising on the outfield during Yorkshire games and we were all relieved that he made a full recovery.

Richie's performances, understandably, did not reach the levels that we had hoped. Many a time he was asleep in the dressing room just before he was due to bat, desperately trying to preserve his energy for a long innings. He spent all his spare time resting and midway through his first season he admitted that the only visitors he had had to his home in Adel, on the outskirts of Leeds, were a couple of Jehovah's Witnesses.

To add to his exhaustion, he was not always entirely suited to slow, low English pitches, which limited the effectiveness of his trademark shot – the exciting square slash on the offside. A record of 1,247 championship runs at 33.70 was not about to single-handedly thrust us to the top of the table, but behind the scenes Richie was providing just the experience and know-how

Richie Richardson did so much to kick-start my England career. Here we are enjoying a singalong during the West Indies' 1995 tour of England.

that we had lacked for so long. We never lost our respect for him.

The turning point of my career – perhaps even my life – came against Hampshire at Southampton. I had bowled well in Hampshire's second innings, but I was beginning to flag and Shaun Udal struck me in quick succession for two straight fours. We were desperate to take the last couple of wickets, and leave ourselves enough time for a run chase, and Richie couldn't hide his irritation. Normally, he was very sensitive to Martyn Moxon's authority as captain. There was no way that Richie would ever try to pull rank. But on this occasion he ran over from gully to give me a kick up the backside. 'You have the ability, man,' he kept saying. 'You have the strength, man, just bowl fast, man.'

There had been times in the past when I had whipped up some speed – notably my five wickets against Lancashire at Scarborough two seasons earlier – but my body had not been strong enough to stand the strain. More often than not, the next match my energy would have deserted me.

But my fitness had improved more than perhaps I realised. I had spent one winter working on the motorways, anxious for alternative employment in case my cricket career collapsed.

Soon after meeting my future wife, Anna, I had improved my diet and begun to work out at the gym at regular intervals. With Richie's insistence that it was about time I bowled fast, suddenly it all clicked into place. At twenty-two I had finally learned my trade.

Wisden records that Yorkshire won that match at a canter. It also states that my first sixteen championship wickets in 1993 cost 35.50, and that, after regaining my place in the side due to an injury to Jarvis, I took thirty-nine more at 21.74. Clearly, a breakthrough had occurred, and Yorkshire felt the fruits of it against Somerset at Taunton when I took 7 for 42 to bowl us to victory in the second innings, returning ten wickets in a match for the first time in my life.

I felt that I had been building up to that day for some time. Still buoyed up by Richie's words, I had a clear picture of what I wanted to be – an out-and-out fast bowler with a yearning to experiment. Alongside a few fast yorkers, I was not afraid to slip in a few off-cutters, a bouncer, or a slower ball, and as my confidence soared, I bowled better and better.

I'd taken some stick from the travelling Yorkshire Press corps for being too expensive, and I took the chance to impress on them that my style had changed. No longer was I trying to become a safety-first English-style seamer, intent on bowling maidens, but too often sending down easy half-volleys. That was just not in my nature. I was now an out-and-out strike bowler, a habitual experimenter. My job was to take wickets; if I failed to do that over a run of three or four games then that was when I deserved to be criticised.

Esso's daughters nicknamed me 'Dazzler', and when I asked why, they explained, 'Well, you dazzle a lot.' Some of the Yorkshire lads started calling me 'Nugget'. Even my nicknames were improving and Martyn Moxon was impressed enough to tip me for international honours. I also felt part of a younger, improving and more optimistic Yorkshire team. Yorkshire capped me in September, and the following day I signed a new four-year contract. We had remained in the bottom half of the championship during Richie's two seasons, but at last I sensed a way forward.

England took up many of my thoughts in 1994, but I managed to maintain my improvement for Yorkshire, topping the championship bowling averages with forty championship wickets at 21.17. Hampshire have figured positively in my career more than once, and did so again at Headingley in late June.

After my Texaco Trophy debut against New Zealand, I had been laid low with a side strain, and missed the start of the Test series. I was far from confident of my fitness for the Hampshire game, but Moxon promised he would break me in gently. For three overs, I could still feel my side and could hardly have bowled more gingerly. Then, suddenly, the pain disappeared. I ended up bowling fifty overs in the match, taking 6 for 70 in the first innings, including Robin Smith for nought. A Test debut at Old Trafford was only a few days away.

In 1995, for the first time, I was ready to tip Yorkshire for success, suggesting that we could reach a Lord's final and finish in the top six in the championship. We came mightily close, losing to Northamptonshire in the NatWest semi-final at Headingley, and failing to reach the top six in the championship only by losing our final game at Chelmsford. Even so, we finished in the top half for the first time since 1987.

Headingley had not been filled to capacity for a Yorkshire match since the Roses matches of the early 'fifties, but the gates were closed for both our quarter-final against Lancashire and the semi a fortnight later when Allan Lamb played splendidly to bat us out of the game.

Due partly to the influence of Michael Bevan, our latest overseas professional, and not a man to mince words, the belief and competitive spirit of a predominantly young side was growing apace. At the end of the season, Martyn Moxon stepped down as captain, confident that the foundations had been laid, and sensing that it was time for a new voice to be heard in the dressing room. Whatever fate lies in store for David Byas, he has inherited a side of rich potential.

6   Star Tips

Michael Atherton: Team Spirit

Every captain should work to foster a dressing-room atmosphere in which all temperaments can flourish. A good spirit is a vital factor in finding success on the field. Different characters, if well looked after, all have a contribution to make to a dressing room.

Cricket is probably unique in that it is a highly individual sport based within a team framework. The secret is to strike a balance. Free expression and free speech should be encouraged, provided that they do not have a negative effect on the requirements and spirit of the team as a whole. People should be encouraged to say their piece, but it is important that they do so in an acceptable manner and at the proper time.

Individual ambition is no bad thing, but it is important that players do not just want to win for themselves, but for the team they are representing. That is just as true for a club or school side as it is for England.

My advice to all young players is to enjoy your own success, but never be jealous when your team-mates do better. It is a wretched player who secretly wants his own players to do badly, just so he can look a little better himself. Whenever we are successful, we all want our team-mates to share in our delight.

Simple things like applauding a team-mate's fifty or hundred, encouraging players through bad times, or backing up a bowler in the field, all help to boost team spirit. When you feel the rest of the team is behind you, your performance is lifted as a result. Everybody is in it together.

Many England cricketers have been powerful individuals. The likes of Darren Gough, Dominic Cork and Ian Botham have all expressed themselves colourfully. As long as they avoid excesses, their effect can only be positive. Other players are not so flamboyant – Angus Fraser perhaps – but they play an equally valuable role. It would be pretty dull if every character was exactly the same.

Every dressing room occasionally suffers a bad egg.

A good team spirit is essential. Here, I'm having a joke during my Test debut against New Zealand at Old Trafford.

Fortunately, I have not had to endure too many. Such a person might moan about twelfth-man duties, pitch up late to the ground, or be a bit of a prima donna, caring only about himself. If he is a world-beater, he might just about be worth the hassle. Otherwise, the likelihood is that he will do more harm than good. Make sure, above all, that person is not you.

Alec Stewart: Preparation

Proper preparation begins well before the start of the game. Firstly, ensure that you are physically and mentally fit, without which you will never do full justice to yourself. Consider the opponents you are going to face, and how best you can combat them. As a batsman, I like to work out how I am likely to play each style of bowler I am going to face – where I am likely to be able to score off them, and what particular problems I am likely to face. As a bowler, try to become aware of a batsman's weaknesses, and how you can turn this to your advantage. No batsman is infallible; no batsman has a divine right to score runs against a bowler, no matter how much he may seem to be on top.

You might think that you cannot tell how a pitch will play just by looking at it, and that it is a waste of time imagining otherwise. We all get it hopelessly wrong from time to time, but that is no excuse to give up. The more you try to read a pitch – examine its hardness, dryness, how much grass it has on it and so on – the more educated you will become.

Visualisation is another form of preparation. I always stand at both ends before a match, especially if I don't know the ground very well, and make myself feel at home. Make a mental note about which way the wind is blowing, whether the square slopes, the size of the boundaries and so on. If you are a bowler, consider whether you have to negotiate an upward slope to the square. It all helps.

If you turn up in time, loosen up properly, have a net, and some fielding practice. Even in small club cricket, players should be looking to arrive one hour before a game. Wandering up five minutes before the start, and getting out for nought a few minutes later, is a mug's game.

Don't be embarrassed about discussing the game with your team-mates. Encourage your captain to offer a few brief words, putting the match into perspective. It can be done in fun, but it does have a purpose.

Practice nights are also important for any club, but practise with a purpose. Aimless practice just makes everybody bored. Before you set out for a game, check your equipment. Why shouldn't you pack spare studs and laces? Include sun cream and sweatbands in hot weather. Don't be the idiot playing in one black sock and one white sock. Even if you can't play, you can always look the part.

In short, do everything you can to give yourself the edge.

John Crawley: Fitness

Cricket was a comfortable existence for me in my early years. As my career progressed, from Manchester Grammar School to Cambridge University and Lancashire, success generally fell my way pretty readily. Fitness was something that I assumed just happened. I was playing a lot of cricket, I was enjoying myself, and I was still young, so there was no problem. When I made my debut for England, no one could deny that life was going swimmingly for me.

But in Australia, on England's Ashes tour of 1994–5, I was given quite a jolt. I realised that my fitness was not comparable with most other international cricketers of my age. The media began sniping about missed catches in the field, some of them real, some of them imaginary.

There I was, only twenty-three years old, and already not regarded as particularly mobile in the field. Perhaps I spent too much time drinking beer, or eating the wrong foods, as if I was still a student just playing cricket for fun. I had always enjoyed that side of life, and although I didn't intend to give it up entirely, it was time to sort out my priorities.

It was the fitness and dietary advice that I received from Alan Watson, in Hammersmith, that put me on the right track. He set out an exercise programme designed to improve my strength, speed and mobility. Once I became fitter, I began to value how much better I felt, and did not want to lose it. My weight fell by nearly a stone in no time at all. People began commenting about how thin in the face I looked! As a Test batsman I need a certain kind of stamina – one that prepares me to bat for six hours, not bowl flat out for a much shorter timespan. Individual needs should therefore influence exactly what training programme you should follow.

Even in Australia, I felt reasonably OK, but my inability always to maintain peak concentration for long periods proved that my fitness levels were insufficient. If a long session in the field leaves you under par when you go in to bat, you will under perform as a consequence.

Many of the advantages that I have gained through improving my fitness are available to players of all ages and all levels. If as a batsman you are struggling against a seam bowler, recognising that he is beginning to tire brings you confidence that you will soon be able to turn things in your favour.

If you are fit, then both your body and your mind are better attuned. Your mind is not under pressure, trying to flog a response from an unwilling body. Nothing comes entirely naturally – even for the most talented, easily fit young sportsman or woman. Some of us have to work harder than others. But, to some extent, all of us have to work.

Graeme Hick: Outfielding

There is a temptation, especially in club cricket, to regard a spot of outfielding as a chance for some rest and recuperation: a bit of a daydream, and a gaze at the scenery, while someone else does the hard work for a while.

It's true, up to a point, that fielding in the deep does not possess quite the same intensity as, say, slip fielding. But without the necessary concentration, you will become a liability to your side.

Always expect the ball to come to you, even if it seems an age has passed since you last fielded a ball. Maintain an interest in the battle of wits between the batsman and bowler; as soon as the batsman shapes to play a shot you should be able to assess what his intentions are. Don't wait until the ball is halfway towards the boundary before setting off in pursuit.

Once the ball is struck, concentrate on the ball and nothing else. If the ball is on the ground, never take your eyes off it, and beware of bobbles or awkward bounces. Attack it as fast as you can, gather cleanly (preferably with two hands) and generally aim your throw just over the top of the stumps.

If the ball is lofted towards you, focus on it as early as possible and, by assessing its arc and its speed, calculate its likely landing point as soon as you can. Get into position quickly and, if you have time, adopt a strong, steady position with your head still and underneath the ball.

When catching a skier, I prefer to position my hands just above eye level. That gives you the best chance of assessing the ball's flight. As you cushion the catch, your hands will drop towards your chest.

Tidy throws are always important, even in routine situations. Just as a fast bowler has every right to demand an accurate return as he walks back to his mark, so a wicketkeeper deserves the same respect. It is an exhausting job, and it is made far worse if throws are forever scuttling in front of him, or forcing him to back-pedal furiously. Good team players throw in with far more consideration that that.

Throwing is a weakness of the English game. In first-class cricket, it probably owes much to the huge amount of matches we play, with a sense of staleness encouraging a sloppy approach. Club cricketers often play on cramped grounds – far smaller than their counterparts in other countries – which rarely demand a strong arm.

There is a technique to throwing which budding young cricketers should learn just as avidly as the techniques of batting and bowling. I was lucky that it always came naturally

A neck-jarring catch on the third man boundary at Lord's during the 1995 Test series against the West Indies.

to me. My upbringing on a farm probably helped, because physical work was never far away.

Learn to throw over the shoulder, which generally offers greater distance and doesn't lead to tennis elbow like its under-the-shoulder counterpart.

Practise with a couple of baseball mitts. Stand about thirty yards away from a team-mate and exchange throws as fast and accurately as you can. Gradually increase the distance of your throws. Done regularly, that will keep your throwing in shape. No one wants to be picked out by a batsman as the fielder with 'no arm'.

Graham Thorpe: Close fielding

If you try to maintain peak concentration every second when fielding close to the wicket, you will probably be carried gibbering from the field long before the end of the innings. One of the keys to close fielding is the ability to switch your concentration on and off as the situation warrants.

Personally, I get focused when a seamer is about halfway down his run, or as a spinner turns to bowl. Immediately after the delivery, I deliberately try to turn off. I have a bit of a chat – anything to relieve the mental pressure. If you like to tell a joke or two, you're better off dealing in one-liners. Long-winded stories have been known to last several overs and might just distract someone at a crucial moment!

At first slip, I watch the ball all the way from the bowler's hand. But when I first began at Surrey, I often fielded at third slip, where the different angle makes it more sensible to concentrate upon the end of the bat. What you do at second slip is really a matter of personal preference. When slipping, stay still and low – don't rise to your feet as the bowler delivers.

Don't spread your legs too far apart, and stand on the balls of your feet – not on your heels. If you start in the right position, there is more chance that you will end in the right position.

Practice is a vital part of slip fielding. Every repetition will sharpen your reactions and attune your mind to the need for an instant response. Slip catches are often taken subconsciously, and the first thing you know is when you get up off the floor with the ball in your hands. When your brain for some reason doesn't pick up the message (perhaps because your concentration was wandering), you often have the embarrassment of never moving a muscle as the ball speeds to the boundary.

If you drop a catch, you are immediately at your most vulnerable. Everybody needs a little mooching period, as they consider what might have been – especially if the batsman is someone like Brian Lara! – but it is vital that you keep your mind on the job.

The most important thing to stress at short leg is to wear the necessary protection. No one questions the courage of many old-timers – most famously, Brian Close – to perch at short leg without a helmet. But I would advise every youngster always to wear a helmet and box without exception. There is no future in taking unnecessary risks. If you realise you have forgotten any protective equipment, stop fielding there until you can go off the field and put it right. If your confidence is still low, and you want to wear shin pads as well, don't let anybody talk you out of it.

Helmets are not always regarded as essential in first-class cricket on the offside, at silly point, but the horrific injury to Nick Knight while fielding there against the West Indies last summer warned of the dangers. Young players, especially, have every right to demand protection.

At both short leg and silly point, make yourself very small. Some fielders put their hands on their knees to give them more stability, and so that they won't flinch. I prefer to have my hands off my knees, and to ensure that my weight is tipped slightly forward.

Close fielders square or in front of the wicket have a right to expect a minimum level of accuracy from their bowlers. Whenever I've felt like an Aunt Sally, I've soon kicked up a fuss!

Robin Smith: Courage

I never thought much about courage. I guess you're either born with it or not, although if you make it to Test level you're likely to have plenty of it.

I have grown up in an age where fast bowling, and especially short fast bowling, has been an accepted part of the game. Helmets came into cricket in the late 'seventies because so much bowling was intimidatory and if players were to survive injury to the head they had no alternative but to wear them.

In all honesty, I have always enjoyed fast bowling – the ball whizzing past my nose wakes me up! – and being such a strong cutter I feel confident of scoring. Some of my best Test match innings have been against the West Indies and I'm sure that the reason for my relative success against them is that I relish the contest.

The most important things are: getting into line, so you are behind the ball in defence; standing up to everything they throw at you, so that the respect becomes mutual; and remaining positive, however tough it seems, because you can't afford to miss the few opportunities you get to score runs.

Only twice in my career have I been physically threatened. Once was on a bad pitch at The Oval when I called for a visor on my helmet against Waqar Younis, and the other was at Edgbaston last summer when another bad pitch encouraged Ian Bishop and Courtney Walsh to bowl very dangerously. I'm proud of the innings I played at Edgbaston . . . courage was needed there all right.

In the next Test at Old Trafford, Bishop hit me in the face. It was quite a shock and I shall wear a visor for evermore now. I thought it might be difficult to come back after the injury but it was OK. I guess you like the challenge or you don't. No

Fast short-pitched bowling soon tests out a batsman's courage.

question, though, the key is guts and courage against the quicks. Look at Michael Atherton – he's the perfect example.

Mark Ramprakash: Concentration

There are many different aspects involved in trying to achieve good concentration.

The first is physical fitness. Modern cricketers have to give this area a great amount of effort and attention. Being physically strong and healthy not only gives you the athletic edge in performance, but will help greatly in maintaining concentration for long periods of time.

Practising hard in the nets can also help concentration skills. By repeating and working at good technique, things such as knowing where your off-stump is, keeping your head still, and nimble footwork should come automatically in the subconscious when batting.

In the build-up to a match, many top players will take time to visualise themselves out on the pitch performing well. They try to imagine the atmosphere, see themselves taking guard, and scoring runs.

For every individual, there is a unique balance between mentally preparing for peak performances on the day and perhaps going too far, becoming too tense and so inhibiting natural strokeplay.

When walking out to bat, it is very important to try and relax. Of course, everyone has to be focused and pumped up to do well, but relaxation is a key factor to good concentration. Remember to enjoy the moment. Try not to think about scoring one hundred. Relish the challenge.

Many batsmen set themselves little targets like getting off the mark, and then counting in tens. During a long innings things may not always go smoothly and you may struggle with your timing. At these times, keep it simple, ticking over with singles, and remembering the importance of playing 'one ball at a time'.

Finally, probably the best piece of advice is also the simplest: concentrate on watching the ball!

Jack Russell: Perfectionism

Perfection is something worth striving for, even though it may not be achieved all the time. Human beings make mistakes, but if they have worked ceaselessly to achieve their maximum potential, then no one can fault them. If you dedicate yourself to getting the most out of your ability, you can walk off the field with pride. Whatever fate brings your way, you will never have a guilt complex at the back of your mind that perhaps you should have tried harder.

The most important thing to maximise your potential is to focus your mind. Decide upon your ambitions and go about them with true determination. Whether you want to be a batsman, bowler or wicketkeeper, if you want to reach the top, you must gear your life to it.

That means getting the right amount of sleep, and the right amount of food. It means getting fit – and staying fit. Once you reach a certain level, it can often mean turning down a night out with the lads. All along the line, you will have to make sacrifices, and remind yourself that you are chasing better rewards. Do not delude yourself – if you are below par either physically or mentally, you will not achieve the results you want.

Perfectionism is about understanding your own game and what makes you tick. But it must be kept in perspective. Errors will occur, and it is important to train yourself to deal with them. The last ball must always be put behind you, whether it was a good shot or bad shot, great ball or lousy ball, superb catch or embarrassing miss.

Mistakes can prey on confidence, while successes can give you too much of a buzz so that your concentration is broken. Perfectionists should not let success or failure affect their attitude and approach. The past provides lessons which must be studied, but should not be allowed to affect how well you play in the present.

As a youngster, I used to watch Alan Knott, the former Kent and England wicketkeeper. The man was a genius – the greatest wicketkeeper-batsman who ever played the game – but he practised and practised every aspect of his cricket. He did not assume that because he was a talented player everything would just drop in his lap. That taught me a lot. If he did it, we all can.

Mike Watkinson: Versatility

It is common for players to be pigeonholed from an early age. From the moment a young player takes up a bat and a ball, coaches are eager to assess where his talent lies.

But don't be rushed into specialising too early. If you feel you have the ability to bat, bowl and field, don't neglect any of your talents. Explore whatever avenue you can – then if things don't work out you always have something to fall back on.

There are countless examples of players whose careers have developed in a way that they might not have imagined.

The South African, Brian McMillan, signed as an overseas player for Warwickshire as a medium-quick bowler, but made his mark that season primarily as a batsman. Without that batting skill, he would have been dismissed as a failure. Bob Woolmer, now South Africa's coach, began life for Kent as a number nine batsman, but worked his way up the order so successfully that he batted for England at number three.

Kim Barnett, at Derbyshire, was a leg-spinner who turned into a batsman. Richard Blakey's batting potential won him a Yorkshire contract, but he kept his wicketkeeping in trim, won England honours in India as a wicketkeeper-batsman, and increasingly at Yorkshire his 'keeping has become the dominant side of his game.

As a youngster, experiment with as many bowling styles as you can. Pupils at Priory School look on while I show them how to bowl an off-spinner.

My own career is also a case in point. When I left West Houghton in the Bolton League, Lancashire did not hold my batting in particularly high regard, but I knew that I had runs in me somewhere and gradually clawed my way up the order. And the fact that I never abandoned my off-spin, in favour of seam-up, led on the wrong side of thirty to England recognition.

Most of us have our favourite fielding positions, but it is not always possible to specialise. The prevalence of one-day cricket, in particular, means that close-to-the-wicket fielders have to be able to field in deeper positions. Borderline decisions in team selection are often decided in favour of the best fielder; this aspect of the game must always be taken seriously.

It is always important to recognise the different qualities of the players in your team, and play accordingly. If your batting partner is more forceful than you are, then you may be at liberty to play the anchor role, confident that your styles are complementary. If that is what the situation warrants, that is all well and good. But occasionally, you may have to force the pace for the good of the team. There is no point complaining that it is not your style – you have to make the adjustment. You have to be versatile.

Richard Illingworth: Competitiveness

There is never an excuse when playing cricket for losing interest or 'jacking' a game in. If you can't play competitively as a matter of course, then you might as well not play at all. You are only making a fool of yourself and the game.

Competitiveness should be your constant rule. Take practice, for instance. It might sound selfish, but you should practise basically for yourself.

When I bowl in the nets, I don't deliberately bowl half-volleys to help a batsman get into form. They know me better by now than to ask me to do that. I practise to get myself into rhythm and to convince myself that I am dropping the ball into the right areas. The last ball I want to get into the habit of bowling is an over-pitched delivery which is likely to go speeding off towards the boundary.

If batsmen want half-volleys then they have to try to use their feet to try to manufacture one. It is tougher, and therefore better, practice for them, too. They should be able to hit a half-volley with their eyes closed. If you insist upon bowling at a batsman's weakness then that should give them the opportunity to improve their technique, or at least learn how to mask their deficiencies.

As a batsman, don't be disturbed by the fast bowlers who glare and curse at you. Aggression is part of their game. Don't feel inferior, and don't flinch. If you are easily intimidated, you can't call yourself truly competitive.

Some people wrongly assume that competitiveness is just about showing hostility to an opponent. The truth is that it should influence every area of your game, including planning.

Every time you see a batsman, examine his grip. If it is closed – that is, angled towards his body – he might favour the legside. Memorise where he scores most of his runs. Does he prefer the offside or legside, or behind or in front of square? Then do your best to drive him to distraction. If he likes short bowling, for instance, never give him the merest sniff of a scoring shot behind the wicket. Make him get fed up with the sight of you.

Even log where members of your own side score their runs, because you never know when you might play against them in the future. All sides change personnel quicker than expected. I keep a mental log of my opponents. My memory is pretty good when it comes to batsmen . . . and to bowlers who break my fingers!

On one occasion, playing for Worcestershire against Glamorgan at Abergavenny, I dismissed Viv Richards, the former West Indian captain, only to be told that I had 'ruined the game'. The suggestion was that because Richards had been dismissed, Glamorgan would lose interest in a run chase. I swore at the suggestion and ended my bowling spell at the end of the over. I get equally angry when cheap runs are deliberately given away to set up a declaration and a run chase. I despise that sort of cricket. Give them nothing – that's my motto. Why not make it yours?

Dominic Cork: Confidence

There are two types of confidence – outward confidence, which does not mean very much, and inner confidence, which means everything. Those who think that all they need to develop is a loud mouth and a big strut, and success will automatically come their way, might be in for a rude awakening. It might fool a few opponents for a while, but there is little point in boasting about how good you are when, deep down, all the usual doubts and insecurities are welling up. A few failures and all those brave predictions will begin to ring hollow.

Confidence, in essence, stems from a true and lasting belief in your own ability. It requires self-reliance, a certain boldness, even impudence. There is no more impudent shot than the reverse sweep, which is why it takes a confident player to attempt it.

You can achieve nothing until you identify what you want to achieve. Once your intentions are decided, never underestimate your own talent. Some good young players might never fulfil themselves because they just lack confidence – maybe the club captain doesn't rate them or their dad once joked that they would never be any good. That can be a terrible waste.

Confidence brings so many benefits, in all walks of life. As a sportsman, it helps you maintain your rhythm, both physically and mentally. The edge to the wicketkeeper because you are tense and uncertain can become a beautifully middled cover drive with more self-belief. When you feel well, you often play well.

It is amazing how well you can do when you feel relaxed. That is why sides often stage an unexpected recovery when they are in a hopeless position. The fact the position seems so

My he-man pose to Ricky Ponting during the first match of the 1994–5 Ashes tour is partly in jest, but it also lets him know who is boss. A bowler's confidence is never higher than when he's just taken a wicket.

hopeless eases the pressure and they play better as a result. Then, the moment that they think they have a chance, the pressure returns. Then, unless they reach new heights, their challenge so often comes to an abrupt halt.

Many Test players use visualisation as an aid to confidence. To prevent doubts welling up before you bat, think positively about how you can beat your opponents. Visualise success, never failure. Never allow yourself to be daunted by a situation, but relish the challenge you are about to face.

Confidence is easy to maintain in a run of good form. But the real test of character comes when things aren't going well. That is the time when it is important to keep faith in your own ability.

Nervousness shows up in so many ways. The batsman who rushes out to the crease is often keyed up and so not as likely to do well. Viv Richards used to walk out to bat with a calmness and a swagger, giving the impression of total self-belief.

And remember, it is not about telling everybody else how good you are, it is a matter of convincing yourself.

Angus Fraser: Perseverance

The longer my career has gone on, the more I have come to realise that things go in cycles. Some days nothing goes your way, at other times you have the luck that makes you some sort of hero. But overall, if you are a reasonable player, things will even themselves out.

However, you don't get that luck if you throw in the towel whenever things begin to go badly. Even though you are convinced it is not your day, even though as a bowler you have flogged yourself into the ground on a flat pitch for no reward, you must keep putting in the effort. If you give up too easily, then on the good days you will achieve less than you really deserve.

Bowlers should expect life to be hard work. Batsmen should accept that first-ball dismissals happen to everyone. The secret to all the bad times is perseverance. When cricket kicks you in the teeth, get up and kick it back again.

Bowling is a long haul. As you improve in standard, so the pitches tend to favour batsmen more and more. The methods that worked under heavy cloud cover on a typically green club 'seamer' are suddenly inadequate when the pitch is bare and the sun is climbing higher in the sky. But you must always tell yourself that it doesn't take much for your luck to change – two bad shots, two good balls and an 'iffy' decision and you suddenly have a five-wicket haul.

Perseverence shows up in different ways, depending on the type of player. For me, perseverance means sticking religiously to a good line and length in the belief that I will eventually force a mistake. Goughie, by contrast, relies on mixing things up, and catching people out with an unexpected delivery. If he bowls a slower ball and it is hit for four, it doesn't mean that it will be the last one he ever bowls.

There are very few players, even at Test level, who consistently look unbeatable – although Brian Lara's 375 in Antigua came close! One ball is all it takes for a batsman to get out. Similarly, a batsman perpetually struggling against a bowler knows that eventually he will be taken off, either because he has tired, or the captain fancies trying something else.

Perseverence also involves thinking positively. If a batsman is giving you a hard time, maybe think about giving him a single to starve him of the strike. Consider changing your field placings – I don't like having a sweeper on the cover boundary, but if a batsman is murdering me, there comes a time to change tack. Batsmen might change their guard, or tell themselves to get on to the back foot a little more. Above all, keep going.

Mark Ilott: Pressure

It doesn't matter how much you train, how much you plan and how much talent you possess – if you can't handle the pressure, you will never succeed. The average player who can perform when the pressure is at its highest is worth his weight in gold to his captain.

There is a great tendency to rush when a match reaches a critical position. In a pressure situation, I try to slow myself down mentally. I make a point of checking my field, and sometimes confer with my captain. It all helps to keep the nerves in check. It is vital to have in mind exactly what sort of delivery I want to bowl. At the end of my run I take a deep breath, and concentrate entirely on the ball I want to bowl.

I try to shut out all the noise around me, whether the crowd is cheering me for all they are worth, barracking me, or baying for my blood. If the match is on TV, by that time I have probably long forgotten it is there. That's when I've got to hope I don't do something silly like pick my nose in close-up! The only time that TV can create extra pressure is at the start of a match when things are a little more low-key and there is chance to reflect.

Sometimes I might try to crack a bit of a joke to relieve the tension. It makes me feel better, although it doesn't always go down well with some of my team-mates. Some of them might be thinking, 'Get your mind on the job,' but it is my way to make the moment easier to handle.

Always try to be aware of your team-mates' reactions in such circumstances, and what mood best suits them. Some bowlers starting the last over with six runs needed to win might welcome lots of geeing-up. For every bowler who will welcome a joke, there is another one who will be deadly serious. Others just want you to shut up. Each is trying to cope with the pressure in his own way.

If I'm fielding at Essex when Mark Waugh or Ronnie Irani are bowling, I've learned to keep my mouth shut. Ronnie gets very fired up and needs to be told that he is bowling well. When the match goes down to the wire, he is very single-minded. Mark Waugh is an extraordinarily talented player who often seems oblivious to pressure and, like all the Australian Test players, he is not one for cracking at the wrong moment.

If you are not afraid of failing, then more often than not you will succeed. If you feel that you hardly dare let go of the ball, you are hardly likely to come out on top. Learn from your mistakes. When things do go wrong, don't dwell on them morbidly, but try to work out what went wrong, and consider how to put things right next time. The fear of failure lurks at the back of every cricketer's mind. That is why players who seem oblivious to pressure – such as Ian Botham – become national heroes. Always tell yourself it's your day. Play naturally, and let the adrenalin flow.

Often when a side is in a difficult position, it releases the pressure and allows them the freedom to stage a recovery. I remember batting with Ronnie Irani in a Sunday League match against Somerset when we needed about fifty runs off the last seven overs, with little batting to come. We told ourselves that we could win the match, and did. But it was only when we needed two runs off the last over, and we realised that we should win it, that the pressure began to bite, and things became much harder.

Lancashire's victory against Worcestershire in the Benson & Hedges Cup semi-final last season was another case in point. Even against a side of Lancashire's batting depth, a Worcestershire win seemed virtually inevitable. Instead of abandoning hope, Lancashire's lower order batted with the freedom of underdogs, and gained a momentum that Worcestershire were never able to break.

Never abandon hope. Pressure does strange things to people.

Devon Malcolm: Fast Bowling

Quick bowling is the most individual talent in cricket. That's why if I had to give one piece of advice to a young lad aching to become a fast bowler it would be, 'Do what feels good.' Not the most technical advice in the world, perhaps, but if your body does not feel comfortable with what you ask it to do, your chances of doing the business will not be very high.

Understanding the basic action is necessary. But once that has been established, just concentrate on accelerating through your run-up, hitting the crease at speed, and propelling that ball as fast as you can. It will soon become clear whether you have the raw materials to become a fast bowler.

Every great fast bowler is different. For every one like Dennis Lillee, a man blessed with a great classical action, there is someone else who is much more unorthodox. Jeff Thomson, Lillee's hunting partner in the great Australian side of the 'seventies, favoured a slinging action that nobody would ever have tried to coach into him. But Thomson was one of the fastest bowlers in history and, at his peak, terrorised nearly every batsman who faced him.

Just look at the differences in styles. The West Indians, Joel Garner and Curtly Ambrose, gained much advantage from their height. Malcolm Marshall scuttled through the crease at breakneck speed. Colin Croft rocked wide of the crease with an awkward splay-footed action. Yet all were born with the same talent: the ability to propel a cricket ball at speeds around ninety mph.

The problem for a teenage fast bowler is that once he gets to a certain age he is surrounded by coaches telling him to change that, and do this, rather than just let him bowl. A lot of coaches try to turn every fast bowler into Richard Hadlee, the essence of a master craftsman, rather than just let them enjoy the game and thrill in their particular blessing.

Often, bowlers without a classical action, who are persuaded by coaches to learn the error of their ways, break down with knee and back problems. Would these injuries have surfaced had they been left alone? In some cases, perhaps they would. But in other cases they break down because they are trying to do something which does not come naturally to them.

England tried to change my action at the start of the South Africa tour last winter. They had good intentions, but I'd just

Adjustments in a fast bowler's action must always be made with great care. My front-foot position was altered last summer after the double fracture which cut short my tour of Australia. Peter Lever, England's bowling coach, and the Yorkshire and England physio, Wayne Morton, discuss adjustments with me at the Headingley indoor school.

come back from a serious knee operation, and I was approaching my mid-thirties. I'd also taken 9 for 57 against South Africa at The Oval on my last appearance against them, which had given me a psychological advantage. My action has never been perfect – coaches make much of my tendency to drop my left shoulder in my delivery stride.

Bowling is a tiring job. I wasn't identified as a possible England player early in my career, so I wasn't overbowled as a youngster. Don't let anybody do that to you. Refuse the extra net session if you feel too exhausted. Don't always agree to drop your pace and become net fodder. Beware of too many indoor sessions, especially in inferior sports centres, where the jarring on the knee and back can do damage. Concentrate on quality, not quantity. Above all, build up your hunger.

Develop a training programme, but only after taking advice from the professionals. Sit-ups done badly, for instance, can do more harm than good – they are less likely to strengthen your abdominal muscles than wreck your back.

Above all, don't bowl through niggling injuries. Get proper advice and get it early. You have only one body. Treat it with the respect it deserves.

Peter Martin: Seam Bowling

There is an abundance of qualified coaches, and cricket manuals, available to pass on the basic methodology of seam bowling. Don't regard it all as a great secret available only to the chosen few. The basic techniques of seam bowling – such as how to grip the ball – are easily understood and available to everybody. The sooner you try to put them into practice, the better.

That said, I'm a great believer in leaving young bowlers to develop naturally as much as possible. There are great dangers in trying to radically change a natural action to make it textbook perfect if that natural action has been functioning perfectly well.

You can always refine an action, to gain extra efficiency, but coaches are increasingly wary these days of changing things too much. If a bowler has a special skill at fourteen, there is an argument for leaving that talent well alone. Many promising bowlers have suddenly lost everything and eventually given up the game. Altered actions can look wooden and manufactured.

Budding seam bowlers should remember that they are still growing, and that they should not put their bodies under too much strain for fear of prolonged injury. Overbowling is a problem for many youngsters as they try to balance demands by different clubs, schools and age-group sides. Set yourself a limit, and don't do an excessive amount of bowling indoors, where jarring on hard surfaces can cause injury problems.

One of my basic intentions as a seam bowler is to create pressure. Occasionally, you take a wicket with a 'jaffa' that you happily tell yourself that any batsman in the world would have found unplayable. But your 'jaffa' often misses everything.

I reckon that ninety per cent of batsmen are dismissed because of pressure. Basically, that boils down to bowling as many 'dot balls' (balls that your opponents fail to score off) as possible. Try to relate it to how you feel as a batsman when you haven't scored for a while. Increasingly, you are tempted to do something rash or impatient. You begin to fear that you are costing your side a chance of victory. Any bowler who can put a batsman into that frame of mind is a winner.

It is important for a bowler to take advice primarily from one or maybe two people. Find someone who you feel happy with and stick with him. Particularly when you are just starting out, it's a mistake to collect conflicting advice from every different source and then try to stick it all together. That is just a recipe for confusion.

Peter Lever has always been a fund of good advice for me. He left Lancashire when I was eighteen, but he had given me a sound basis. As England's bowling coach, he was on hand again in South Africa to discuss my form. Paul Allott, the former Lancashire and England seamer, is another ex-player whose advice I trust and value.

Darren Gough: Enjoyment

By now, most people know my attitude. However you spend your life, you might as well try to enjoy it. I'm lucky to play cricket for England, something that millions have dreamed of apart from me, so the least I can do is go about things with a smile on my face.

It takes far more muscles to frown than it does to laugh. How often has someone told you that? Yet look around you every day of the week and count the miserable faces. Some people might have cause to be sad – personal misfortunes, perhaps, ill health or unemployment. But when I'm playing cricket for England, I am experiencing a thrill allowed to so few, and millions of people are cheering me on. Why shouldn't it give me a kick?

There is a theory that talented young cricketers don't get the chance to learn to love the game these days. The minute they show any promise, they are packaged off into representative sides, and from there into county nets or cricket academies. Coaching begins at an increasingly early age. In no time, sport has become an examination subject more than a recreation.

Fortunately, I managed to cram in a couple of years at Monk Bretton, in the Pontefract section of the Yorkshire Council, before I started on the treadmill, so I sampled the love that thousands of amateur players at small clubs have for the game. Cricket takes many hours to reach a conclusion, which leaves plenty of time for laughter amid the competition. Every young player should enjoy that humour. Try your utmost while you are on the field, and examine every way to improve your game, but when it is all over, try to laugh at both success and failure. That will make your experience so much more worthwhile.

Not appreciating the lighter side only creates unnecessary extra

Relaxing during practice in Perth at the start of the last Ashes tour.

pressure. Everybody knows players who never fulfil their potential because they are too screwed-up about success and failure. We all want to achieve, often badly, but try to keep it in perspective.

Test cricket, of course, is no laughing matter. It is played under tremendous pressure. Close-ups of players on TV often reveal the stress that they are under. Modern demands are more intrusive than ever, but eventually a new generation of players come along who are able to cope with those demands. I believe that the likes of Dominic Cork, Mark Ilott and myself are determined to enjoy international cricket whatever fate might lie in store.

Look around you at those older, or less fortunate. You are lucky just to be able to dash around the field, take a flying catch, slam a quick 50, or bowl a bouncer. Relish it, and remember it. Laugh about it, and love it. If, at the end of it all, your talent shines through, you may one day play for England. If not, with the right positive attitude, there is still endless satisfaction to be had.

7   Getting in Shape

'*D*arren Gough's future as an England cricketer began to take recognisable shape the day he turned his nose up at a hamburger.'* That was how Peter Johnson, in the *Daily Mail*, explained my transformation from a run-of-the-mill county cricketer to an England fast bowler.

In fact, my England call-up inspired all sorts of imaginative tabloid headlines. While the *Mail* settled upon 'BURGER KING'S SLIMLINE TONIC . . . GOUGH MOVES FROM FAST FOOD TO THE ENGLAND FAST LANE,' the *Daily Star* blazed an even more uncomplicated trail: 'GOUGH THE SCOFF: I WAS A YORKSHIRE PUDDING.' The *Yorkshire Evening Post* liked that headline so much that they adapted it the following day, under the headline of 'HOW GOUGH THE SCOFF BECAME DYNAMIC DARREN.' All that after one brief interview. You could definitely say that my first meeting with the England Press corps had left me with a lot to digest.

I'm not ashamed to admit that there was a time when I was not fit enough to do myself justice as a professional sportsman. What I can take pride in is the fact that I changed my ways before it was too late.

Football was my first love, and it was football, and more precisely Rotherham United FC, that first took a look at my shape and judged that I was never going to make it as a professional.

I represented Barnsley Schools from under-11 to under-16 level, and loved nothing more than to sit in the centre circle and spray passes around all afternoon long. I was skilful, but when it came to tackling back, or making energetic forward runs, my enthusiasm declined. I lacked the drive to make much of an effort, and just contented myself by dreaming that my ball skills would see me through. In England, of all places, that is never the case.

I used to tell myself that I was a Glenn Hoddle type of figure, although others might prefer to say Jan Molby. Hoddle was one of my boyhood heroes. He was a superb passer of the ball, but fell from favour with England – unjustly so –because of his fell from favour with England – unjustly so – because of his limited involvement in the physical side of the game.

After leaving school, I became a YTS trialist at Rotherham for three months, and came under the eye of Phil Chambers, the youth team coach. Phil had a useful career in the lower divisions, and knew what commitment was required to make the grade. What he made of a rotund and confident young lad who would never turn up on a Wednesday, because he knew that was the day when training was the hardest, I can't imagine.

On Wednesdays, rather than over-exert myself, I used to wander into Barnsley with my mates. Suggestions that we would eat and drink ourself silly are wide of the mark – I never had enough money for a McDonalds. We used to wander around the shops, doss around, and just pass the day the best we could. If I stayed at home, I would lounge on the sofa, watching the TV.

My dad kept telling me to get my finger out, and warned me that I was wasting my ability, but I just used to tell him not to worry. I always had confidence in my ability, and I thought I would make it in the end. But I'm not boasting, not for a minute. The main reason that I sorted myself out was that I met Anna. It is amazing what falling in love can persuade you to do.

I first met Anna on the Costa del Sol in the winter of 1991–2. As soon as I had returned to England, I rang her up, and after eight weeks I proposed to her. I normally have a habit of leaving things until the last minute, but nobody could accuse me of dragging my heels this time.

That winter I had grave doubts about whether I would make it as a county cricketer, or even whether I wanted to. I had begun to realise that I might need another job – and quickly – so I took the chance to work on the motorways for Tarmac and Reymac, learning to do everything from road-safety duties to resurfacing. A lot of it was heavy work and the Gough body began to take a bit of a battering. As a professional sportsman, I wasn't going to complain that I was finding it hard going, but it made me wonder about the standard of my fitness.

Jokes that my favourite delivery used to be a takeaway pizza are not far short of the mark. In Anna's eyes, I was a typical single bloke, going out to the pub with my mates and eating junk food. She knew that I wasn't going to get very far unless I changed my habits.

Put simply, my problem was that I liked many foods that weren't particularly good for me. That hardly makes me unique.

Getting in shape has meant fewer packets of crisps and more fresh fruit.

Cans of pop, chocolate bars and fish and chips are the favourite food and drinks for millions, yet they can cause havoc with your fitness if they are eaten to excess. I don't think that I was ever a porker – I don't hold the Barnsley record for the number of curries in one night, or anything like that – but I had some work to do

Anna does not eat red meat, so when she began to take charge of the cooking, the change to a chicken, fish and pasta diet, with heaps of fresh fruit and vegetables, soon became the norm. I was surprised how much I enjoyed it, and knew that it was precisely the sort of diet that I should have been following for years. I even took an active interest in cooking. The takeaway curry houses and kebab centres had to brace themselves for a fall in profits.

By the following winter, we had moved into a flat on the outskirts of Barnsley, and while Anna was at work, I was too embarrassed just to laze around all day. I started working out on most days, two hours at a time, at the Metrodome gymnasium in Barnsley.

Oddly enough, Anna had been more fitness-conscious than

me. She used to work out at the gym three or four times a week, and I was not going to let her outdo me. Once I started, I began to take pride in the fact that my body was in better condition. The training began to give me a bit of a buzz, and I became quite addicted to it. Instead of wondering whether I could whip up the energy for another training session, I soon began to look forward to it. These days, with spare time so precious, we've invested in a mini-gym at home with weights, an exercise bike and a step machine.

When I went back to Yorkshire, under Anna's influence, for pre-season training, my weight had dropped from 13st. 10lbs to 12st. Once everybody had got over the shock, Wayne Morton (who has since become England's physio as well as Yorkshire's) advised me to put on a few more pounds so that I didn't lose any power. I've settled on about 12st. 7lbs and these days keep to it pretty consistently. It's a long time since I've heard my old nickname of 'Guzzler'.

BRIDGING THE GAP

These days we take for granted untold benefits which were unimaginable not so long ago. Satellite television, CD players, convenience foods, faster and sleeker cars, and central heating are just a few luxuries that millions of people enjoy. But when it comes to physical fitness, modern lifestyles have caused many problems. The gap between the fit and the unfit has never been as great.

Fitness used to happen naturally. My parents' generation walked long distances to school, and even further to Saturday night dances. Without central heating, they tended to live a more active home life, often just to keep warm. Even if they had television, it did not come with a collection of automatic handsets which enable you to zap the controls without leaving your armchair.

Work also tended to keep more people fit. Twenty or thirty years ago, many employees stayed naturally fit with heavy manual jobs. Coming from Barnsley, I don't need to be told about the physical strength needed to work down the mines. The power of some of those miners was awesome. But most of those mines have closed. Unemployment is high, and those fortunate enough to find fresh employment often discover that many jobs these days require far less exertion. Working on the office computer, for instance, is not about to improve your aerobic rate.

As well as the temptation to laze around these days, we are forever tempted by the sort of fast foods our parents dreamed of. For my mum, processed peas were a technological breakthrough, and a Wimpy bar was one of the seven wonders of the world. Now we are assaulted constantly with images of every type of junk food imaginable. We can hardly walk a yard in the High Street without being assaulted with images of fizzy pop, ice cream, chocolate and cheeseburgers. Like it or not, we are living in Big Mac country.

That causes problems. Teenagers will not like to admit it – perhaps too many conversations with Wayne Morton, the Yorkshire and England physio, are beginning to make me sound like an old bore – but obesity rates among the under twenties are at an all-time high. I recognise that I was overweight at the start of my sporting career and it might have cost me the chance to play for Yorkshire and England.

At a time when general fitness is collapsing, sport is making heavier demands on players than ever before. Athletes continue to break records as training routines and techniques reach new heights, premiership footballers possess a stamina far beyond their predecessors, and cricketers dive around in the field where once they merely waved the ball on its way to the boundary. Sport is big business, and expectations are at an all-time high.

That has caused an enormous gulf which many young players fail to cross. Gone are the days at the highest level when a naturally fit youngster could wander up to his chosen club, amble a couple of times around the field, and be pronounced perfectly fit for the task. Now even a respectable level of fitness is likely to be regarded as inadequate. Achieving the minimum acceptable levels is a tough task.

Some budding sportsmen and women never cross this widening divide. Some fail to cross it without serious injury. I've heard countless theories about why so many modern fast bowlers break down with stress fractures of the back before their careers have hardly begun – including coaching techniques, indoor training and too much cricket at a young age. But the fact that their bodies are often not fit enough to deal with the demands placed upon them is often a root cause of their problems.

Fitness used to just happen. Now it takes a definite decision to get in shape. Parks and cycle tracks are full of joggers, health and fitness clubs are springing up on the edge of town centres. It might not seem cool to be seen to take your body seriously. Fitness clubs for many youngsters might be too expensive. But it is far easier to stay fit than to get fit.

If you have an inkling that you possess a sporting talent, don't hesitate to get yourself fit. Schools are beginning to take PE and Leisure more seriously, and not before time. I used to dislike Chemistry and still had to go to the lessons. I don't see why those who hate PE should not experience the same difficulties. It's all good character-forming stuff!

Viv Richards, the former West Indies captain, is scathing about English attitudes. He argues that our failure to produce many fast bowlers is nothing to do with a greater natural ability for producing raw speed in the Caribbean. He puts it down to the unwillingness of young English players to commit their bodies to a demanding all-round training programme. It is far easier to bowl medium-fast on responsive English pitches.

Stay fit and you will never regret it. You will be sharper in

Getting fit need not be a bind. Approached properly, it can make you feel healthier, happier and more relaxed.

both mind and body. We all laughed at Graham Gooch on tour when we were woken up some mornings by him pounding up and down a fire escape. No one was more adamant than Goochie that fitness had to be worked on more with every passing year. The result is that he played cricket for England at forty while many begin to falter ten years earlier. He has developed such good habits that he will probably remain fitter than his contemporaries well into old age.

In Australia, there is a clothes chain called Country Road – and decent stuff it is too. Goochie was a regular visitor. One day during the Ashes tour of 1994–5, he nipped off to stock up on a few items. While he was gone, Keith Fletcher, then the England team manager, needed a word with him.

'Where's Goochie?' asked Fletch.

'Oh, he's gone up Country Road,' someone said.

'What?' exclaimed Fletch. 'He's not gone jogging again, has he?'

In the following pages, I've tried to explain the basic dos and don'ts involved in healthy eating, and physical and mental fitness. No one wants you to become someone you are not. But you can only be wholly satisfied if you can say you have done everything to fulfil your ability. You can't maximise your potential if you haven't had any sleep the night before, if you're 'pogged up' with pie and chips, or if you're out of shape.

Before we get underway, thanks are due to Wayne Morton, the England and Yorkshire physiotherapist, who knows more about my fitness and eating habits than anybody, and who has helped me to put the following advice into action.

EATING HABITS

I heard a story once about a Sunday League junior footballer in a league in Yorkshire. He lived in a traditional family where the Sunday dinner – roast brisket, Yorkshire puddings, mashed potatoes and vegetables, with an apple crumble to follow – had been the norm for as long as he could remember. Any attempt to change the family's eating habits was bound to cause problems, so not wanting to appear ungrateful, he ate the lot. Often, the meal finished around 1.30 p.m. before his father rushed him and his brother to the ground in time for a 2.30 p.m. kick-off.

Many of you will know similar stories. If it is not the player turning up to the ground fit to burst, it is the member of the team who always has to have a pie and a couple of pints before the start of the game. Literally, at every level of every sport, eating habits like this hand the opposition the game on a plate.

Scientific evidence suggests that meals should be completed between two and three hours before the beginning of a match for maximum energy benefit. But cricket makes such advice extremely hard to follow, especially at first-class level, where the games can seem everlasting.

Nancy Doyle became so famous for her meals in the players' dining room at Lord's that she was awarded the OBE. I realised the enthusiasm for Nancy's cooking when I made my Yorkshire debut at Lord's against Middlesex, and I was soon tucking in with the best of them. Her bacon sandwiches, steak and kidney pies and apple pies were legendary. Many people joke that her magnificent three-course dinners made Mike Gatting the man he is today. Many people will also say that it didn't do the likes of Ian Botham any harm, and it didn't, but Both was an extraordinary player with extraordinary needs.

Dietitians connected with other sports, where meals are planned to the minutest detail, would be astonished that cricketers consider such a substantial meal in the middle of a day's play. In no other top-level sport do people eat to perform. The habit probably began when first-class cricketers were much more poorly paid than today, and valued the financial saving that a large meal at 1.15 p.m. would bring. Then, if they got sidetracked in the pub during the evening, and never got round to eating, they thought that no great harm was done.

Wayne Morton will tell you that, by the time the next generation of young cricketers break through, cricket's breaks for such large meals will probably have died out – even the pasta dishes that have become a regular feature on the first-class circuit. Intervals are increasingly being used to consider tactics, stretch, rest or to restore fluid levels.

Obviously, professional cricketers have to eat at some time during the day. It is important to get up in time to eat a good breakfast. That used to mean a traditional fried English breakfast every morning, and although that would now be frowned upon, the body can handle that as long as it is in moderation.

Alternatives these days, though, centre around cereals, toast, fruit, scrambled eggs and yoghurts. This means that by lunchtime, if you expect to have little to do for the rest of the day, you might feel in the mood for another meal. But if you are batting, or planning a long bowl, then you should be able to shun more food without too much bother.

Habits vary. Martyn Moxon, the former Yorkshire captain, often lunches very lightly – nothing more than a ham and coleslaw sandwich, perhaps. Jack Russell has the most unusual habits of all –he thrives on Weetabix, and even likes the milk to be put on it about ten minutes before the interval. Like many cereals, it is high in fibre and carbohydrates, and has a good cross-section of vitamins and minerals.

These days, England have an array of snacks around the dressing room as an instant energy source – things like carbohydrate bars, fruit-and-nut bars and jaffa cakes. It all helps the players, although when the bag of miniature doughnuts were passed around in South Africa, the chairman of selectors, Raymond Illingworth, had to show a lot of willpower to keep his waistline in check.

That leaves the evening meal, when you should be eating something balanced and nutritious. Who said 'Pot Noodle'? The time it is eaten doesn't matter too much, although it's best to give the 12oz T-bone a miss last thing at night, especially if you are playing the following day.

Nutrition

In the past year, various studies have 'proved' that sugar is good for you, half a bottle of wine is quite beneficial after all, and red-meat eaters consume less fat than vegetarians. Other studies warn us that many things can have dire consequences for our health. Immediately these studies are announced, another study concludes exactly the opposite.

Every interest group lobbies on behalf of its own products, and every supermarket shelf heaves with health claims for hundreds of products. It is so easy just to curse the lot of them, and eat whatever takes your fancy. But there are simple guidelines that you can follow without becoming obsessive about your diet.

Not so long ago, nutritional advice concerned itself largely with how much you weighed. That was understandable after the Second World War when food was scarce and rationing books were still in place. Fast foods were still not invented. But advice now centres upon the types of food we eat, and also maintaining the correct levels of fluid. The principle is that, although you can run a car on diesel or petrol, it runs better on petrol; the same applies to the human body.

Carbohydrates are an important energy source. Foods rich in carbohydrates include sugar, bread, potatoes, rice and pasta, as well as all cereals, fruit and vegetables. Because fruit and vegetables have a high water content, the carbohydrates in them are quite diluted, and you can therefore eat large quantities without too much risk of putting on weight. However, this also means that they are not the most efficient energy source. Bread, cereals, pasta and rice are more concentrated in carbohydrates.

Fat is found largely in all animal products – including meat and eggs – nuts, fried foods and milk. This is the most concentrated source of energy, which is why it brings the risk of putting on weight. Over-indulgence in fats is these days generally frowned upon.

Food also has other important uses. Milk is a supplier of calcium and meat, fish and cheese are rich sources of protein. Citrus fruit will top up your vitamin C.

Coffee and tea both contain caffeine, which might give you an early-morning boost, but too many cups and all those toilet visits will threaten your fluid levels!

In simple terms, the best advice is to eat a balanced diet. And, if your weight fluctuates too wildly, make some sensible adjustments. In that, very little has changed.

Fluid

The experience of the Australian batsman, Dean Jones, when he collapsed during the 1986 Madras Test, after playing one of the most heroic Test innings in Test history, warned that the immense commitment demanded of modern players could put their health at risk. Last winter, in Australia, England's Graham Thorpe also suffered from dehydration and required drip treatment in hospital after batting in extremely hot temperatures in Brisbane.

Constant medical supervision is essential, and the ways of protecting players from dehydration are gradually changing.

Maintaining fluid levels in hot and humid climates has long been recognised as essential. The question is how best to achieve it.

Ten years ago, the stress was placed upon bottled water. Tap water is too risky in many parts of the cricketing world, particularly in Asia, and the mass of fizzy drinks on the market, all possessing a massive sugar content, tended to blow you up if you drank too much, or too quickly. Clean water was one of the simplest and best things for a player.

For many club cricketers, not facing quite the same demands, it still is. Batsmen playing long innings, or fast bowlers operating for lengthy spells, should make sure that they take in plenty of fluids. There is no reason why a bowler should not have a water bottle down at third man to grab a drink at the end of an over. Neither should a batsman automatically be prevented from grabbing a quick drink during an innings just because the drinks interval is not due. Umpires, understandably, do not welcome too many unnecessary interruptions. But when cricket is played in hot temperatures, protecting a player's health should be the priority.

When I bowled in Brisbane – the most humid of Australia's

Dehydration is one of the greatest dangers when playing cricket in hot weather. Graham Thorpe takes more fluid on board after a demanding net session in South Africa.

cricketing cities – on the last Ashes tour, I lost three pounds of fluid. I didn't bowl too many deliveries before I was looking red in the face. If I had not rehydrated quickly enough, I could have been in big trouble. Leave it too long, and when the stomach does receive liquid it can go into spasm. Wayne always likens it to a hard ground after a prolonged period without rain – it is much harder for the water to soak through.

It became fashionable for a while to use salt tablets. That was a way of adding extra sodium to the fluid to help the body to take it up. But often the resulting mixture was too strong and the results were not particularly good.

In recent years, we have benefited from the advent of modern high-energy sports drinks. They are designed purely to allow the body to rehydrate. They possess minerals and electrolytes, basically the things your body loses when it sweats. Drinking these during a strenuous match will be of more benefit than pigging yourself on another can of fizzy.

The latest development amounts to virtually a meal in a drink. One sachet can be the equivalent of a three-course meal, without the disadvantage of loading a player up with too much bulk halfway through a day's play. England experimented with a variety of these drinks in South Africa last winter. Who is to say that they didn't help Michael Atherton maintain his energy while playing his brilliant backs-to-the-wall innings for more than ten hours to save the Johannesburg Test?

Wayne is confident that these drinks can be a massive boost to the body. You are able in one fell swoop to take on the carbohydrates and minerals required to see you through a day's play. One drink is equal to more than four platefuls of spaghetti. It has always broken all sport's rules when cricketers sit down to a substantial meal in the middle of the day, and such developments suggest that the days of the steak and kidney pie and chips regime and apple crumble are numbered. It's a good job, though, that the carbohydrate drinks did not come in while Gatt was still a Test player. Can you imagine the size he might have been if he had tried everything!

Dieting

Many people who want to lose weight quickly opt for some sort of crash diet. I always have visions of fat folk munching sticks of celery, which has so few calories that you actually burn up more calories in the effort of eating it. The ultimate weight-loss food!

Dieting works on simple principles. If over-indulgence causes you to put on weight, then reducing your food intake will solve the problem.

But rigid dieting is generally not a sensible solution for an active sportsman. Often the body reacts to receiving less food by conserving energy wherever it can, with the result that the individual can become slower, less active, and less alert. That's not a whole lot of good if you are about to play an important match. If you are exercising hard at the same time, then the body simply is not receiving enough food to cope, and the danger of injury increases as a result.

If you need to lose weight, a change of diet, rather than simple dieting itself, is a better place to start. That and a well-planned programme to improve your fitness.

Alcohol

Sports writers often bemoan the fact that things aren't what they used to be. Time was when they could lean against a carefully chosen bar in the evening, and before too long, an entire team of sportsmen would have wandered in for several pints and a natter.

Life has moved on. Players are more cagey about what they say, and to whom, and the levels of drinking have definitely fallen even in the few years I have played first-class cricket.

Although he would never go out of his way to recommend it, Wayne sympathises with the view that alcohol, in limited amounts, can make a positive contribution to a player's psychological state. It is more and more difficult these days for international sportsmen to escape the high levels of stress which their sport brings. A couple of pints, or a glass or two of wine, does assist relaxation, and therefore recuperation, of both mind and body. By helping your state of mind, you can also be helping your physical fitness.

That does not give every young cricketer an excuse to rush off and drink the town dry, especially if you are underage. Drinking binges do nobody any good.

FIT FOR THE TASK

Choosing to get fit is only half the battle. Deciding how to go about it is more complicated than ever. Before you know it you might be swamped by many phrases that you have never heard before or, if you have, you are not entirely sure what they mean.

'Sport-specific warm-up rates', 'cardiovascular fitness', 'anaerobic endurance levels', 'isotonic resistance', 'isokinetic training' and 'ballistic flexibility' might all rear their ugly heads. Just reading that might make you desperate for a fizzy drink, a bag of crisps and a lie-down in front of *Neighbours*.

It all goes to show that 'getting fit' is not as simple as it sounds. What sort of fitness do you mean? A marathon runner might be lacking when it comes to flexibility. Similarly, just because you can run a hundred metres quicker than most does not prevent you from being incapable of lifting all but the lightest weights.

Until you know what you want, you can't get what you want. It's time to sort out the specialist jargon and develop a clear and simple idea of how you can best get yourself fit for the task.

Time to pick Wayne's brain again! Fitness can be divided most simply into the following categories: **(i) Stamina, (ii) Speed** and **(iii) Strength and Power**. All are important in playing cricket successfully. Here's how you can improve them.

Stamina

My eyes glaze over when I hear people spouting terms like 'aerobic exercise', 'cardiorespiratory fitness', or 'cardiovascular fitness'. But don't lose heart. What they are referring to is stamina. For youngsters with mediocre fitness, stamina is the first priority.

Simply, the greater your stamina, the more efficient your body is in supplying oxygen to hard-worked muscles. Jogging is particularly useful for stamina-building for cricketers because it most accurately reflects the movements needed during the game. In one-day cricket, in particular, you are persistently on the move.

But if you find jogging the most boring activity on earth,

then cycling, skipping and swimming are also excellent substitutes, as well as endurance exercises like sit-ups and press-ups. Walking is useful, too, although not necessarily if the walking is linked to a Saturday night pub-crawl.

Demands upon stamina can be made in different ways. Devon Malcolm or myself might need energy in relatively short bursts, whereas Richard Illingworth or Phil Tufnell have had many days when they are expected to bowl from dawn to dusk. Ask us to exchange roles and, because our bodies are not used to such demands, we would all struggle.

Stamina depends upon improving the efficiency of the heart and lungs. That is why gymnasiums are strewn with charts showing various levels of heart rate. Anybody can jump on an exercise bike, pedal for half an hour with a grimace on their reddening face, and probably do themselves some good. But, like Wayne always tells me, a more calculated method will bring greater dividends. 'Please engage brain before moving,' and all that stuff.

The charts say that you should exercise at between sixty to ninety per cent of your maximum heart rate. The medical types generally calculate that maximum rate as 220 beats per minute, minus your age. For those without either a calculator or A-level maths, here is a rough guide. Those aged between fourteen and twenty-one should aim for a heart rate between 125 and 180 beats per minute. The fitter you are, the closer you can aim to the higher number.

But a word of warning, as in all cases: if you feel any dizziness, or pain, stop immediately.

Many gymnasiums have special heart rate readers. Otherwise, it's a case of 'fingers on the buzzers', the buzzer in this case being your pulse. If you can't find it for all the fat on your neck, then perhaps you should take things easy for a while!

Speed

Every outstanding cricket team needs its share of quick players. Matches can be won and lost by batsmen haring singles, by cover fielders swooping and throwing in one movement to run out a batsman who is well set, or by slip fielders whose reactions are so sharp that they make difficult catches look simple.

You might realise from an early age that you will never quite

Great fielders
are blessed with
both speed of
thought and
speed of action.
To take this
'chance' last
summer, they
would also have
needed to be a
magician!

make it as a first-class cricketer. But that does not mean that you will automatically fall below the required standards in every facet of the game. There is no reason, particularly, why club players blessed with agility and rapid reactions should not achieve fielding standards comparable with many professional players.

Another lesson, hot from Wayne's notebook! Speed depends upon two different responses: how quickly you react and how quickly you move.

Reaction time is often greatly underplayed but, especially for close fielders, it is essential. There is nothing more frustrating for a fast bowler than to find the edge of the bat only for the fielder at slip or gully not to move a muscle. In many cases, that has to be because his concentration has been allowed to lapse.

Outfielders also benefit from a rapid reaction time. How many times have you seen a skier head towards the boundary, only for the fielder to set off in pursuit when it is too late. You might be able to run the 100 metres quicker than anybody in your team, but if you are dozing around when the ball begins to head in your direction, the chances are that you will not put that talent to good use.

In a long game like cricket, concentration cannot be consistently maintained at peak levels. The knack is to switch concentration on and off as required. There is nothing wrong with having a laugh and a joke between deliveries as long as your mind is on the job as the bowler begins to run in. It might even refresh you, and make your concentration even sharper.

Try also to read and understand the game, wherever you are fielding. If you are fielding at deep square leg, and the batsman is about to cut a wide long-hop then there is very little chance that the ball is going to find its way to you. But if you sense that a batsman is shaping for a pull shot, then it is time for your brain to be on red alert. Taking an active interest in the game will teach you to recognise situations and your brain will respond all the quicker as a result.

But there is little point in having sharp reactions if your movements are sluggish. How quickly a player moves is what most people consider when they are assessing speed. Trying to improve your speed is straightforward – you need nothing more than a pair of training shoes and a stopwatch.

Attempt regular shuttle runs between ten and fifty metres, trying to match as closely as possible the sort of situations you will face during a game. If there are a few team-mates about, introduce a ball so that you can practise your picking up and throwing. Invent whatever rules you wish to give the session a more enjoyable, competitive edge.

Michael Atherton's running between the wickets has improved dramatically in the past year or so. He was advised that he was slowing down too early to turn for a second run. Now he tries to hit the return crease at a higher speed, and has been surprised how much faster he has become as a result.

As your speed increases, so should your agility, although there are many ways in which you can work on this too. One of the simplest and most effective exercises is much loved by the Australians and was a feature of their pre-match routines during our 1994–5 Ashes tour. It goes like this: a fielder sprints in to collect a catch delivered from about twenty yards away, and immediately returns it to the stumps. He continues his run forward, receiving a second catch from about ten metres out. This again is returned on the run, and the exercise is completed as he collects a third and final catch only a yard or so away from home. It looks – and feels – exhausting.

Strength and Power

The worst possible advice to give a young person who is seeking to get fit would be to start by lifting heavy weights. In the first instance, stress should be placed upon stamina, speed and agility. From the age of about fourteen, lifting light weights can help your cricket, but only under careful supervision, and to begin with no more than a couple of times a week. Larking about with weights is one of the stupidest things you can do.

Once again, it's easy to get bogged down in all the jargon. Two descriptions that crop up time and again: *isometric exercise* and *isotonic exercise*. Isometric exercise involves pushing against an immoveable object, such as a wall. Isotonic exercise involves the use of moveable objects such as barbells and dumbbells, and it is many of these which will probably be of most benefit.

General weight training exercises are best explained by qualified staff at your local gymnasium. But as a budding cricketer, you should also wise-up about certain exercises that will be of particular benefit to your sport. Enquire about exercises that simulate the actions needed in the sport. For

An arduous workout during England's last tour of Australia.

example, a bowling pulley can be used to simulate the movements involved in bowling a cricket ball.

Weight training is still regarded suspiciously by many cricketers. Just one look at a superheavyweight collapsing under a bar every Olympic Games is enough to put you off for life. And Martyn Moxon, when he was Yorkshire captain, added to his reputation for being unlucky with injuries when he fractured his wrist while exercising with light weights in the Headingley gymnasium. So it is important to remember a few safeguards:

- Always warm up properly.
- Always ask advice when unsure.
- Train under supervision of properly qualified staff.
- Do not overtrain.

Warming up

For much of cricket history, warm-up exercises were largely overlooked. If players did attempt any sort of warm-up, it involved a quick knock-up in the nets and a stretch to tie their bootlaces. The less committed preferred a fag and a cup of tea in the corner of the dressing room. Lunchtime exercise involved the crossword, the racing guide, and the loan of a pair of binoculars to search for the prettiest girl in the ground.

Nowadays, stretching exercises are all part of the daily routine as players try to guard against injury. Stretching before a game prepares the body for the task. Stretching after exercise is also beneficial in improving a sportsman's flexibility.

Outside the professional game, it is all too easy to wander on to the field without any proper warm-up. For one thing, while

Stretching exercises are often overlooked, but they are vital in protecting against unnecessary injuries.

half a dozen members of your club might claim to be an expert in the art of the outswinger, not one of them will have the slightest opinion on how best to stretch a calf muscle. But, at whatever level you play, you should take the chance to warm up properly. You are simply looking after your body and you'll be grateful for it in the long run.

Bad stretching exercises can put strain on your joints. So study the accompanying drawings and take care to warm up in the manner that Wayne recommends to the England and Yorkshire players.

ALL-ROUND (Fig. 1):
Position: lie on back, feet and arms outstretched.
Exercise: stretch body as much as possible.

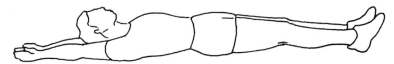

Fig. 1: All-round stretch.

ARM (Fig. 2):
Position: kneel on all fours, arm extended.
Exercise: pull shoulder back.

CALF (Fig. 3):
Position: lean against a wall, with your foot pointing forwards.
Exercise: bend leg, keep heel on ground. Push forwards and downwards with hip.

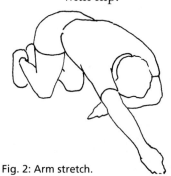

Fig. 2: Arm stretch.

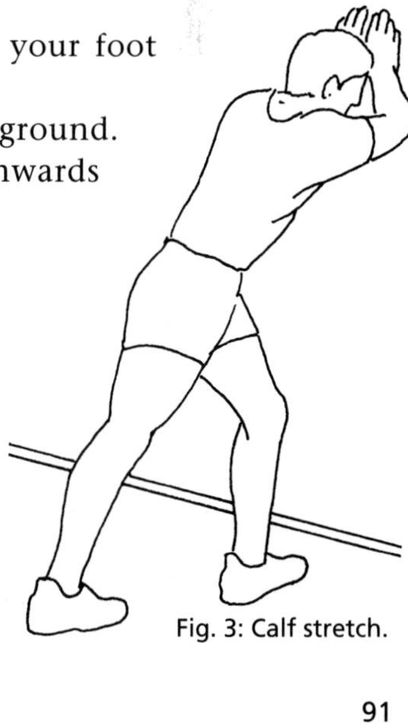

Fig. 3: Calf stretch.

GROIN (Fig. 4):

Position: sit on floor, legs folded, feet together.

Exercise: gently push knees outwards and downwards.

Fig. 4: Groin stretch.

HAMSTRING AND LOWER BACK (Fig. 5):

Position: sit on floor, feet together and legs straight.

Exercise: stretch forward towards your toes.

Fig. 5: Hamstring and lower back stretch.

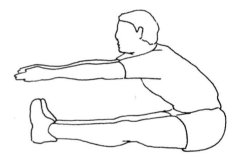

HIP (Fig. 6):

Position: crouch on one knee, with other leg stretched out behind.

Exercise: push hip forward.

Fig. 6: Hip stretch.

SIDE (Fig. 7):
Position: stand upright, feet apart.
Exercise: bend to side. Hold for a few seconds.

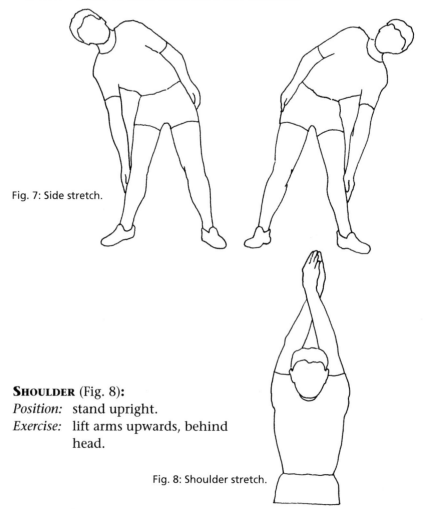

Fig. 7: Side stretch.

SHOULDER (Fig. 8):
Position: stand upright.
Exercise: lift arms upwards, behind head.

Fig. 8: Shoulder stretch.

Mental fitness

I would be the first person to admit that my form against the West Indies last summer was disappointing. After a colourful and exciting start to my Test career, my lack of success caused some commentators to suggest that I was beginning to believe my own publicity. Even some ex-Test players cagily suggested that might be the case. It was sad that they, in particular, should have made such a judgement, as they have had first-hand experience of how injury can affect a player's outlook.

In Australia two winters ago, everything I touched turned to gold, and my confidence was high as a result. Everybody commented upon my optimistic approach to life. But my tour was cut short when I fractured my foot while bowling in a one-day international in Melbourne, and the injury preyed upon my confidence long after I had been pronounced fit the following summer. I badly wanted to play again for England, and believed I was fit enough to do so, but it is not always possible to banish nagging doubts about your state of health overnight. Negative thoughts were lurking around every corner. It was a recipe for disaster.

If the after-effects of serious injury can affect a player's mental well-being, then so can general lack of fitness. If your body is not in tip-top condition then, however talented you might be, your mind is also liable to respond sluggishly. Peak physical health encourages mental sharpness. That, in turn, breeds lasting confidence and self-belief.

Players who feel good in themselves are more likely to pull out all the stops. They might take a storming catch, summon up the strength for one more over when the pressure is at its height, or possess enough concentration to bat all day.

And self-belief is everything. Viv Richards, the great West Indian batsman, used to claim in his heyday that his younger brother has always possessed more cricketing talent. Yet constant comparisons with Viv wore him down and, after playing for Antigua, he abandoned the game. He did not have Viv's mental strength.

Spectators will often chide a player for lacking enthusiasm. Occasionally, they might be right to suspect a lack of professionalism, or basic love of the game, lies at the heart of it. But there are many times when that player might be carrying an injury, or be mentally drained from a long journey from a late finish in a one-day match the night before. In such cases, mental health can come under great strain. It's an old cliché, I know, but a healthy body really is a healthy mind.

EQUIPMENT

Equipment has come a long way since the ancient club bag with its collection of sausage gloves, strap-on box and 2lb 2oz bat with its annual coat of linseed oil. These days, the choice is mind-boggling, and making the correct decisions can help to tilt the balance in your favour.

Try to choose a bat which has four or five even grains running vertically down its length. Lightly oil it if required and knock it in religiously with an old ball, or a special bat hammer, before using it in a match situation. Toe-guards, if you wish, also offer extra protection against splitting the bottom of the bat.

The difference between a dead bat and one which has a sweet middle is the difference between being caught at cover, or hitting the ball over the infield for four. Distinctions in quality, especially at a higher level, can make the difference between long-term success and failure. I have recently concluded a sponsorship deal with Duncan Fearnley for my cricket bats. Duncan is a fellow Yorkshireman, even though his affiliations have long been with Worcestershire, and I'm sure his bats will give me marvellous service.

I use a bat of 2lb 9ozs, which among Test players is regarded as a middle-of-the-road weight. Doug Padgett, the Yorkshire coach, preferred a bat as light as 2lb 4ozs in his playing days in the 'sixties and he constantly criticised the 1980s trend towards heavier bats. Doug used to have a party trick in my early days in the Yorkshire 2nd XI. He would grab hold of a bat and if he didn't like the pick-up, and thought it was just a plank of wood, he used to throw it out of the window.

In one warning, Doug was absolutely right – don't use a bat that is too heavy for you. As well as limiting your cross-bat shots, you will not be able to play with sufficient control. I was twelve years old when my dad bought me an 'Ian Botham Attack'. I was thrilled because of the name – Both had just slayed the Australians at Headingley – but I could hardly lift it. As soon as I went to a proper coaching class, they took it off me because it was far too heavy. I thought, 'Get off, it's my bat!'

When you are starting out, the club bag should be sufficient for much of your equipment. But choosing the correct bat is such a personal decision that you should try to have your own whenever possible. When you are just beginning to learn the game, you don't need to spend £100–150 on a top-of-the-range bat – shop around – but you must feel comfortable with how it feels.

Helmets are here to stay, whether for batting or close fielding. In Australia, I experimented with a helmet made by Open Championship, because it was the first helmet to be approved by the British Safety Institute. If you are going to go to every length to protect yourself, it makes sense for every helmet to have been officially tested.

I'm a big believer in advising young players to wear a helmet, especially against quick bowling. In lower leagues, the bowling might not be as fast but the pitches, equally, might not be as reliable. Anything that helps your confidence has to be worthwhile, and you are drastically reducing your risk of serious injury. If you graduate to a higher standard, a helmet will become commonplace, so why not become used to it as early in your career as possible?

The sweep is being played more and more, as is the reverse lap, even against medium paced bowling. That increases the risk of top-edges into the face, especially on pitches of uneven bounce.

Not every player likes to wear a visor. Robin Smith, for instance, was not wearing a visor when he was struck in the face while batting against the West Indies last summer. He responded by wearing a visor for the first time in his career on last winter's tour of South Africa and struggled to get used to what he sensed was a restricted view. Personally, I like the security that a visor gives me. There is no point having a full field of vision if your eyes are splattered.

Gloves unfailingly attract criticism these days, but the quality of protection has to be the best it has ever been. There are more fractures around these days, but that is not because the equipment is not what it used to be – there are simply more fast and fast-medium bowlers around. Top-of-the-range gloves might seem too stiff, especially for players just starting out, with relatively weak hands, so it is important to consider flexibility. You will not make many runs if you cannot grip the bat comfortably.

Pony, who supply my footwear, are discussing how to design a boot to give me maximum comfort and protection. I've certainly spent some time experimenting with various styles throughout my career.

When I suffered my foot injury in Australia, I was bowling in a fielding shoe, which history suggests was a mistake, and about which the old-timers would throw up their hands in horror. The reasoning was that because I'm relatively small, and run on my toes, I felt happier in a lighter boot.

Once I had recovered my fitness, at the start of last summer, I switched to the cross-trainer, which is halfway towards a

Meeting Harold Larwood was one of the greatest thrills of my life.

(Above) Michael Atherton's defensive technique, shown here in his monumental 185 not out in the 1995 Johannesburg Test, is the bedrock of England's batting.

(Top Right) I don't often bowl in sunglasses, but I did during Yorkshire's NatWest semi-final against Northants at Headingley last summer. After the hoo-ha over whether I was fit to play, some people reckoned it was an attempted disguise!

(Bottom Right) One-day cricket never fails to excite me. An appeal against Jonty Rhodes in the second International against South Africa at Bloemfontein.

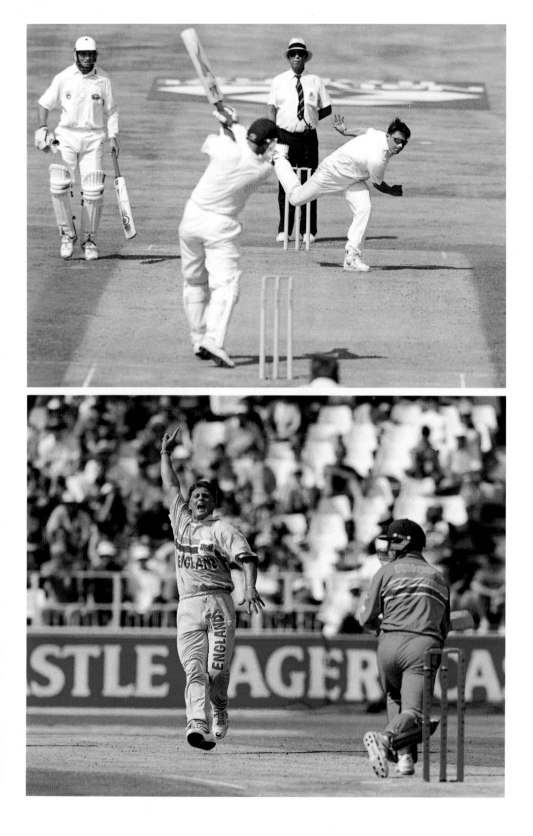

There is nothing better than playing for England.

bowling boot, but although it was comfortable, it still did not give me quite the support I needed.

Since then I've chosen a more traditional bowling boot – the Paceman – which is a tighter fit and gives me more support. That is the boot that bowlers such as Devon Malcolm and Angus Fraser prefer. I took the Paceman with me in Australia but never wore it, which I should have, especially on hard grounds, where my feet suffered more jarring.

One course of action I have decided upon is to have special shock-absorbing leather insoles fitted into my boots. My foot was moulded into a plaster cast to ensure that the insole perfectly suited the shape of my foot. If you have any weaknesses in your feet, extra little bumps can be built in to compensate. If you can only afford one pair of boots – and most amateur players make do with that – my advice is for you to choose spikes over rubber soles.

Take care of your equipment and ensure that it is appropriate to your needs. Last summer I began to use specially manufactured insoles to give myself extra protection.

Another tip young players should always follow is to throw away those thin cotton socks if you don't want to suffer from blisters. Wear proper thick cricket socks, or walking socks.

The most vital advice of all is when you are batting always wear a box. Cut out the sniggers. Cricket balls can do tremendous damage. Never go out to bat without one.

There are a host of other protective aids, especially at first-class level. As well as pads, batsmen might strap on outer and inner thigh pads, chest pads and arm guards. I rarely use an inner thigh pad because I find it uncomfortable. But after Allan Donald struck me on the inner arm during South Africa's tour of England in 1993, I decided to go out to bat in two arm guards. I looked a bit unusual, but he had showed me how much damage I could do.

Batting while carrying so much 'luggage' can certainly be wearing, especially in hot climates. It's no surprise that batsmen need drinks every half hour to replenish their fluid levels. Doctors always advise regular drinks to avoid dehydration. Spectators who barrack the delays are often sitting under cover having a drink at the time!

Sunglasses have attracted much criticism as little more than a style accessory. There has even been way-off-the-mark talk that Ray Illingworth, as chairman of selectors, has tried to ban them. Odd that, as he wears them all the time! There are only about three England cricketers who are sponsored to wear sunglasses – I have a deal with Oakley – so people can hardly be accused of doing it for the money.

I would never wear sunglasses for the sake of it. They are an absolute must. People wear sunglasses to watch, so players should be allowed to wear them to play. If your eyes are exposed to the sun for long periods, specialists are increasingly insistent that you can do permanent damage to your eyes. Cricketers spend a lot of time outside in the summer months. No one should ask us to put our health at risk.

As well as the sunglasses for bright conditions, there are also the type that enhance light in cloudy conditions. I'm equally convinced that they are a benefit. Occasionally, there are a few players who lazily wear the wrong type for the wrong conditions. They are being unprofessional and, if they drop a catch as a consequence, they are spoiling it for the rest of us.

Sun cream is equally important in sunny weather – and that means England too! Skin cancer is now one of the most common killers in the world, and its effects are rising. I was ignorant about the effects of sun as a teenager. I used to go to Spain with the lads, slap on factor two and burn all day. Now, I know better. Nivea sun creams are constantly on hand in the Yorkshire dressing room. An outdoor life is really enjoyable, but you must be aware of the dangers.

8 Back to School

There are still a few misguided souls who will tell you that cricket is elitist, a game designed as a leisurely pursuit for the gentlemen of the upper classes. I think we can treat that theory with the contempt that it deserves. That might have been true fifty years ago, especially in the South. But nowadays, on the field at any rate, it could hardly be more cosmopolitan, a jumble of accents and attitudes.

One thing is for certain – my upbringing will never be described as elitist. A proud product of the comprehensive system, that's me, an ex-pupil of Priory Comprehensive, Barnsley. If anyone had put a silver spoon in my mouth, or that of any of my friends, we would all have gone into a huddle and decided to trade it in for something more useful.

There is no point denying the fact that in recent years, cricket has come under great pressure in comprehensive schools. In fact, in many areas of the country, it has struggled to survive. Fortunately 'Quick Cricket', of which I am a supporter, is now helping to put things right.

In the name of controlling budgets, cricket squares have disappeared as quickly as cream cakes at a meeting of the Delia Smith fan club. For a time, team games became unfashionable, and all the rage was for individual sports. Too many educationalists have been fond of quoting claims that 'for every one cricketer you can afford to train ten athletes.' So what? You could probably teach a hundred to play snakes and ladders.

Slowly, there are signs that in the comprehensive schools cricket is fighting back. On my last visit to Priory School, I was delighted to hear the head, Duncan Gawthorpe, talk enthusiastically of restoring a proper grass square. Good luck to him.

Other comprehensive schools are also working to protect their facilities. Some are using artificial surfaces, which require little maintenance, and provide consistently safe practice. Badly kept grass wickets do more harm than good. They shake the confidence of young batsmen, who slip into bad techniques in the name of self-preservation. Geoffrey Boycott always talks

Priory School, Barnsley, where my sporting skills first began to branch out.

about 'sniffing the ball' when you play a forward defensive shot. No one is going to do any sniffing if they are in danger of losing their teeth. And fear can take years to eradicate.

Schools are also sharing facilities with the community, which reduces costs. The Sports Council, through the success of the National Lottery, is also part-financing facilities that had seemed out of reach for all but a few. And plans for the restructuring of the English game should see more first-class cricketers passing on their knowledge to schoolkids than ever before.

And where schools are failing to offer cricket to their pupils, clubs are beginning to recognise that they have a responsibility. It is down to them to fill the gap, by running junior sides and offering youngsters a basic introduction to the game. We won't produce top-class Test players just by exciting coverage on Sky TV.

If cricket is seriously to rival football as our national sport, all this and more needs to be done throughout the country.

Such opportunities require a huge amount of voluntary work, and we all know that teenagers are not always the best at saying thank you. Gratitude comes in later life. I can say for sure that without the encouragement of so many volunteers when I was just another slightly flabby, but skilful young sportsman, the world would never have heard of Darren Gough.

All this made me think it was about time I revisited my roots again, so armed with a few cricket pictures for a school display, I made another return to Priory School, which had managed to keep me on the straight and narrow until it was time to leave at the age of sixteen.

I'd always tried to stay clear of the Head Teacher's study. Suddenly, I was being invited into it, without any fear that trouble might be brewing. Or so I thought! The Head, Mr Gawthorpe, certainly caused quite a stir when he produced from his desk my old school reports.

My school record is not too much to write home about: two O levels and five CSEs. In spite of countless well-meant warnings about laziness and failing to achieve my potential, I never managed to commit my mind to the job. I knew deep down that I wouldn't achieve what I should have done, and embarrassment ensured that I never bothered to go back to school to discover my exam results.

Fortunately, cricket gave me an outlet. I'll always be thankful for the opportunities it has brought. But it might have been better if I'd listened to urgings to maximise my potential while I was at school and not just on the cricket field.

Years later, it was fun flicking through some of the comments from my old teachers. Some of them seemed to bear a resemblance to the more critical utterances about my England career. See what you think.

Mathematics: 'A year of two halves,' and 'Often misunderstands instructions because of his tendency to be doing other things whilst the instructions are being given.'

English: 'Extremely talented writer but has periods of coasting when he feels he can sail through with little or no effort.'

Metalwork: 'Good practical work, but must make sure he understands the theoretical side.'

Textiles: 'Needs further practice with the sewing machine.'

Leisure: 'The sensible use of leisure time has never been one of Darren's problems.'

Art: 'Must ensure that his tendency to chatter does not begin to affect his future progress.'

General comments: 'Has his heart in the right place, but is inclined to be flippant over his studies. A very talented all-round sportsman. A career in sport of some description would be ideal. '

When I was younger, there were so many questions I would have liked to ask my favourite sports stars. How did Chris Waddle manage to beat full-backs at what seemed to be such a leisurely pace; did Ian Botham really like a pint or two the night before a big game, and did anyone ever try to make Glenn Hoddle tuck his shirt in?

So while I was back at Priory School, it was a perfect opportunity to put my head on the block. Down in the gymnasium, I was surrounded by young cricketers, just like I had been a few years before, eager to discover a little more for themselves. I've taken the liberty of filling out some of my answers in more detail, but this is basically how it went:

Pupils at my old school take the opportunity to grill me about my career.

Matthew Warzytz: What teams did you play for when you were younger?

Darren Gough: Like most youngsters, I started with my school teams – St Helens Junior School and then Priory Comprehensive. Then my first chance of league cricket came

with Monk Bretton, a little village just north of Barnsley. They also produced Martyn Moxon, so for such a small club they have good reason to be proud of giving such a solid early grounding. I stayed at Monk Bretton for about five years before I joined Barnsley in the Yorkshire League. From there, you know the rest.

Ian Dixon: Who are the comedians in the England dressing room?

Darren Gough: What, besides me? Let me see, who is the funniest? I'll tell you about the Yorkshire dressing room first. Yorkshire hasn't always been famous for a funny dressing room, but in the last few years, it has become much more fun. Paul Grayson is quite a character – things will be a bit quieter now that he has gone to Essex. Peter Hartley as well. He has a dry Northern sense of humour.

In England, it's not so simple. There are a few different characters in that team. They're not all from Barnsley, you know! Dominic Cork is quite perky, and Steve Rhodes used to make me laugh, but if I had to pick one, I'd pick Angus Fraser. You might not think so from watching him on the telly, because he always looks as if his bowling is blooming hard work, which it is. But off the field he has a good sense of humour. A strangely miserable one, too.

There is a lot of pressure and tension about when you are playing for England, so it can get pretty serious at times. You need someone to lighten the mood every so often, otherwise you'd all crack up. There is nothing wrong with a bit of banter now and then as long as you are concentrating when the time comes.

Thomas Rushforth: Was there any conflict between you and your brother, Adrian, when you were young over who was best at cricket?

Darren Gough: No, not cricket. Football, definitely. My success was quite hard on Adrian because he was quite good at sport as well, football especially. When I got the chance to play for Yorkshire quite early, he soon stopped playing seriously.

He was a good player. He captained South Yorkshire at football, and a few clubs were interested in him. But he lost a bit of interest. He also broke his arm when he was younger so his cricket went off a bit then. He still plays football, and cricket now and then, but he could have gone a lot further.

It can be hard for a younger brother to follow someone who

has done well. It's a bit like having a famous dad. It can make things hard to cope with. He is only in his early twenties, so he has got lots of good footballing years ahead of him if he wants them.

Paul Gaskell: When you were good at football as a teenager did you ever think you would play for England at cricket?

Darren Gough: When I was growing up, I would have preferred to play for England at football. That was where my true love lay. I was always better at football as a kid, and with a bit more effort I could probably have made a career for a while in the lower divisions, but that wasn't really very appealing. It was when I left school at sixteen that things began to change. When I started playing cricket three or four times a week, I began to realise that cricket was actually my best sport. I got a YTS contract at the Headingley indoor school and committed myself to cricket so much that I didn't play football at all for three years. I just jacked it in, although I was still a fan.

Ian Dixon: Is Brian Lara the hardest batter to bowl against?

Darren Gough: Yes, definitely. He is not much fun. He is obviously the best strokeplayer in the world, but with him being left-handed as well it becomes even harder. You have to

Brian Lara gets my vote as my hardest opponent. He gave me some rough treatment in England's 1995 series against the West Indies, but I did dismiss him in the Lord's Test, caught behind by Alec Stewart.

alter your action slightly because of the different angle and if you don't get your line absolutely right, he just carts it for four.

David Gower was similar, although Lara has taken it one step further. You just don't fancy bowling when he is batting. If you had any sense, you would try and hide in the field, and hope the captain put on someone else! He tonked me all over in England last summer, didn't he?

Duncan Gawthorpe (Head Teacher): Taking which wicket gave you the most pleasure?
Darren Gough: It would have been Richie Richardson if I had dismissed him in a Test match, because Richie had such a positive effect on my career at Yorkshire. To prove to him how much I had improved would have given me a great lift.

But the choice has got to be when I dismissed Martin Crowe on my one-day international debut. When you are picked for England, you want to make an immediate impact. You never know whether each game might be your last. It doesn't matter how confident a personality you are, you don't know for certain whether you are good enough to perform at that level. To get a wicket with my sixth delivery was a thrill.

Another choice would be David Boon in the first Test at Brisbane in Australia in 1994. It was my first Test wicket overseas and meant a lot to me.

Richard Barraclough: Which has been your easiest Test match?
Darren Gough: Easiest? You don't get many easy Test matches! But the Test where I didn't bowl well and still came out with a lot of wickets was Melbourne in Australia. I didn't think I bowled brilliantly, but I got seven wickets in the match and a lot of kind comments from the crowd and in the media. I probably bowled as poorly in Melbourne as at any time on that tour, but sometimes luck just goes your way, and you might as well ride it for all it's worth.

Matthew Warzytz: Do you still talk to your friends now you're famous?
Darren Gough: I don't deny that it's hard, because I don't live in Barnsley any more, and I have a wife and young family to care for. You spend so much time away from home as a cricket professional that every spare moment with the family is

vital. You can't come home from a three-months tour and tell your wife, 'I'm just off out with the lads tonight.'

But my best friend has always been a lad called Chris Lycett. We've been good mates ever since we fell out in the third year. We had a couple of scraps but since then we've been best mates. He was supposed to be best man at my wedding but he bottled it. I should have been best man at his, but I was playing cricket. Still, the thought was there. But we still keep in touch. I see another couple of people every now and then, but it gets harder and harder to keep your old friends. That's true not just for me, but for millions of people.

Jonathan Bentley: Do you get a lot of people coming to your door, asking you for autographs?
Darren Gough: I did where I used to live. I've just moved to a new house, and already, within the first fortnight, a few people managed to track me down. I don't know how they managed to find me, but they did. I don't mind as long as it is not all the time. I'd have done the same – I'd have knocked on an England player's door and asked for his autograph when I was a youngster. You can't tell people to go away, so I always sign them.

I'm down a fairly private road, which gives me a bit of peace, but I wouldn't say I'm barricaded. There are no plans for electric fences and barbed wire! Hopefully, I'll never take that attitude.

Ian Downes: What did it feel like the first time you walked on to the field for England?
Darren Gough: Without sounding like an old softy, I was quite emotional. On both my debuts, for Yorkshire and England, I didn't exactly cry, but I felt like I was going to. It was the fulfilment of a dream, something to make your bottom lip tremble and your eyes well up with tears. From playing for Yorkshire, I was suddenly in an England dressing room alongside people like Michael Atherton and Alec Stewart. It takes some getting used to. After about ten minutes you begin to feel part of it, and that you belong there. It's vital that you're made to feel at home before you go on to the field. One unsettled player can make the difference between winning and losing a Test.

Neil Fox: Have you got any nicknames with England or with Yorkshire?

Darren Gough: I tend to be called Dazzler, which I quite like. I'm in the habit of signing it occasionally, and I've even called my company Dazzler. It's got no money in it, but at least it has got a name.

On England's A tour to South Africa, Steve Rhodes nicknamed me Rhino, because of the way I came snorting and charging to the wicket. I need a hide as strong as a rhino, too, to cope with all the mickey-taking I get. Since I got into the England side, I've also been called Showman, because the lads reckon I act up a bit on the field.

Lots of nicknames aren't very imaginative. Michael Atherton is called Athers – that's all he has got. Similarly, Mark Ramprakash is Ramps, and Graham Thorpe, Thorpey. Little imagination has gone into those.

When Alec Stewart isn't called Stewey it is probably because the old favourite, Mr Perfect, is being used instead. 'Jack' Russell's nickname is so universal that it is regarded as his real name. When did you ever hear anybody call him Robert?

Angus Fraser mostly gets Gus, which is fairly predictable, but he is also called Donkey. Must be something to do with his appetite for hard work. John Crawley gets Creepy, and Robin Smith is known as the Judge, because his thick curly hair used to look like a judge's wig. Even his wife and his agent regularly call him by his nickname.

Mark Ilott is known on the circuit as Ramble, because he rambles on and on. He is also called Chook and Headless – which has something to do with a variety of chicken.

Corky answers to Snafflers, Shirka, Gorbachev and Golden. Golden Wonder, I suppose – after the crisp packets? The more success he has, the more nicknames he collects. They are like trophies in a way, and it is normally the most outgoing personalities who attract the most of them.

Many nicknames arise during the course of a season but most survive only a couple of days, and then disappear. Quite why some catch on is difficult to say.

David Bairstow, the former Yorkshire captain, was a prolific inventor of nicknames. They tell the story of one day at Scarborough in the late 'eighties when Ian Swallow stood underneath a skier. 'Chicken, George, Swall, Young 'Un,' bellowed Bluey. And that was before the ball had started to come down. Somehow, Swall realised that all four names referred to him and, instead of fearing a mighty collision, clung on to the catch.

Ian Dixon: Do people phone you up to ask you to wear their equipment or clothing?

Darren Gough: I have a clothing sponsor, Pony UK, who own Kickers, Speedo, Head, Lacoste, and Ellesse, so any of that gear I tend to wear. Much of it is the sort of casual clothing I prefer to wear anyway, so I'm perfectly happy with that. My footwear is Pony, who produce probably the best cricketing footwear you can get. They've been very helpful in trying to design a bowling boot to protect me against further serious injury.

Christopher Woodward: When you were at school were you a fast bowler then?

Darren Gough: Well, I was on the way to becoming a fast bowler. When I was at school, I was a bit lazy, as my school reports will tell you. I was really a medium-pacer and I enjoyed batting. But after school my bowling improved and my batting went downhill. Only in the last few years has my batting begun to show signs of improvement again.

Mark Forrest: Do you enjoy playing for Yorkshire?

Darren Gough: I didn't used to. When I first got into the side, it was quite hard to settle in. The average age of the side was about thirty, and for an eighteen-year-old that was a big difference in attitude and approach to have to bridge. But now the Yorkshire dressing room is quite funny. The average age is in the mid-twenties. Many of the younger players, such as Michael Vaughan and Anthony McGrath, have both talent and enthusiasm and you can't ask for more than that. Players are getting younger and younger. I'll probably be out of a job in another five years.

Neil Armitage: Which bowler do you most fear?

Darren Gough: As we don't play South Africa for a while after the 1995–6 tour, I can admit it: Allan Donald, without a doubt. There is nobody any quicker in the world. He mainly pitches it up – he is one fast bowler who still tries to knock your pegs out – but when he does bowl the short ball, he takes some handling. I found that out at Lord's in 1994 when he rapped me on the arm and caused me to retire hurt.

Courtney Walsh also causes me endless problems. He is not as quick as other bowlers, but he comes from such a height that he gets steep bounce, and he is always at you. He never gives you a loose ball to hit.

Craig Gaskell: Many bowlers name Brian Lara as the batsman they most fear. Who would you choose apart from Lara?

Darren Gough: Tough question, that one. The hardest opponent I faced in my first ten Tests was Martin Crowe. What a brilliant player! He is getting on a bit now, but I still think he is one of the best in the world. He is so technically sound. He has held New Zealand's batting together for most of the past decade.

Another batsman I'd choose would be the Australian, Steve Waugh. You always think you are about to get him out, and you are often disappointed. When he comes in, all the England players get particularly fired up. He often gets hit a couple of times, everybody fancies picking up a wicket, but he is rarely as vulnerable as he looks.

Australian batsmen have great stickability. Mark Taylor and David Boon both 'guts it out', hang around and hit the bad ball. Michael Slater and Mark Waugh both love to express themselves and play shots. It gives them an excellent blend.

Thomas Rushforth: What type of game do you like best – Tests or one-day internationals?

Darren Gough: Traditionalists won't be too impressed, but in terms of sheer enjoyment, I prefer the one-day internationals. In Australia, especially, day-night cricket is tremendously exciting – a riot of colour, noise and expectancy.

The day that I fractured my foot, I played in front of 75,000 people in Melbourne, all catcalling and jeering. It was a brilliant atmosphere. Even in international football, you don't often sense an atmosphere like that. When you do well, the ground just erupts and, for an extra thrill, you can relive it all on the big TV screens.

Nothing – apart from perhaps a World Cup final – rivals a Test match for sheer importance, or for proving a player's true worth. County matches must always be respected, because they provide satisfaction for thousands of spectators, and are the basis of our professional first-class cricket structure. But give me a one-day international in Australia every time. I'd love to play in one every week.

9   Dazzler's Skills Factory

BATTING TIPS

The Basics

Before you attempt to emulate Michael Atherton or Brian Lara, it is vital that you get the basics right.

The simplest guide to obtaining the correct grip is to put the bat face-down on the ground and pick it up as if you were handling an axe. This should ensure that your hands are close together in the middle of the handle. Look for the Vs formed by the thumb and forefinger of each hand. They should be in line, halfway between the outside edge and the splice. The back of your top hand should be pointing in the direction of wide mid-off.

Don't grip the bat too firmly or too loosely. Gripping too firmly is the sign of a tense, rigid batsman. Too loose a grip will reduce control and might even cause the bat to fly out of your hands.

A batsman in defensive mood might often have his hands closer to the bottom of the bat. A batsman with attacking intentions, and a liking for the drive, might position them higher, although he will not quite possess the same control.

Practise swinging the bat from the top of the backswing so that ideally it passes over the top of the stumps and invariably comes down towards the ball in a straight line. Playing straight is essential. If you play across the line of the ball, you have no margin for error. The slightest error in timing will prove costly.

The stance is equally important. If you feel uncomfortable, something is wrong. You must have a relaxed, balanced and comfy stance. Other points to watch out for are:

- Balance your weight on the balls of both feet, and bend your knees slightly.
- Point your leading shoulder at the bowler. Occasionally, especially when facing fast bowling, you might feel the need to open your stance slightly.

- Keep your head upright and still, facing the bowler. Your eyes should be steady and level.
- Ground your bat lightly just behind your back toes. The timing of your backswing must be in tune with the bowler's approach. Begin your backswing as the bowler is about to deliver the ball.
- Concentrate and watch the ball!

One to watch: Michael Atherton (England).

THE FORWARD DEFENSIVE SHOT

When: A defensive shot against a good-length ball, on or around the line of the stumps. Essentially, the aim is to survive, and ensure that you are still batting when the bad balls come along. A sound defensive shot can be most dispiriting for a bowler.

How: Thrust front shoulder and head towards the ball. Your front foot follows towards and alongside the line of the ball, pointing roughly in the direction of the shot. Transfer your weight on to your front foot. Front shoulder should point towards the line of the ball, with front elbow bent. Don't lunge forward. Angle the bat slightly downwards.

One to watch: Michael Atherton (England).

THE BACKWARD DEFENSIVE SHOT

When: A defensive shot against a ball just short of a good length, on or around the line of the stumps. Another survival shot. You cannot defend everything off the front foot – the bowler will soon become wise to that and bang the ball in shorter.

How: Move your back foot well back into your stumps towards the offside, with your front foot following. Keep your head and eyes behind the line of the ball. Stay side-on. To keep the ball down, raise your front elbow, and push your top hand ahead of your bottom hand. Slacken your bottom hand so it does not take charge of the shot. Let the ball come to you, and play with 'soft hands'.

One to watch: Michael Atherton (England).

THE FRONT-FOOT DRIVES

There are several variations on the front-foot drive, including:

- **The straight drive:** sends a straight, overpitched delivery back past the bowler.
- **The off-drive:** hit through mid-off against an overpitched ball which pitches around or slightly outside off-stump.
- **The cover drive:** essentially an off-drive, but played through cover or extra cover against a slightly wider delivery.
- **The square drive:** a wider delivery still. Hit square on the offside.
- **The on drive:** punishes an overpitched ball around leg-stump, by driving it between mid-on and midwicket.

Fig. 9: Cover drive.

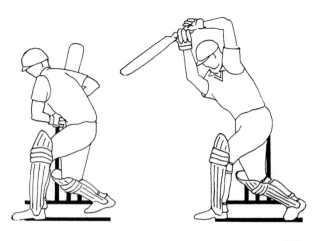

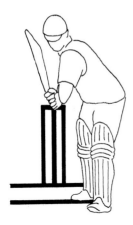

Fig. 10: On drive

- **The lofted drive:** deliberately hit 'over the top'. The ball is lofted over the infield. A Gough favourite!
- **Advancing to drive:** leaving your crease, most often against a slow bowler, to make a good-length ball into an overpitched one

When: In each case, the ball is overpitched – that is, it bounces too close to the batsman, allowing him to drive firmly off the front foot. A ball that bounces just in front of a batsman is called a half-volley.

How: The drive is an attacking shot with a vertical bat. To beat the field you will need a combination of power, placement and timing. Watch out for late movement or deliveries that bounce more than expected. These factors often cause a batsman to be caught at the wicket, or in the close fielding positions.

In playing the front-foot drive, many of the basics explained in the forward defensive shot come into play, although with more attacking intent.

Move your front foot alongside the line of the ball and point your front foot and shoulder towards the direction of the stroke. Push your head and eyes over the ball. Bent front elbow and knees slightly bent.

The wider the ball, the less you will remain side-on to the bowler.

Aim to swing your bat close to your pad, so you don't leave a 'gate' between bat and pad. Allow your bat to follow through, over your front shoulder.

The straight drive can be a very safe shot precisely because you are playing so straight. It is also highly satisfying – sending the ball whistling back past the bowler is one of the most dominating shots in the book.

One to watch: Alec Stewart (England).

The cover drive is regarded by the purists as the most elegant shot in the game. One to bring a round of oohs and aahs on any county ground. Schoolmasters love it!

One to watch: Graeme Hick (England).

For **the square drive**, the ball is wide outside off-stump, leaving little chance of being bowled or lbw. But you are hitting more across the line of the ball than in, say, a straight drive, so your judgement must be spot on. Beware dragging the ball on to your stumps off the inside edge.

One to watch: Graham Thorpe (England).

The on-drive is the most difficult shot for players to master. Many err by playing across their front pad. The trick is to open up your stance, by moving your front foot and shoulder out towards mid-on. That allows the bat room to swing through in a straight line. A drive generally played with a more dominant bottom hand.

One to watch: Sachin Tendulkar (India).

The lofted drive: don't lift your head to try to scoop the ball over the fielders. Keep your head down and, with a flowing, unchecked stroke, allow your arms – not your body – to lift the ball. By the time you look up, the ball should be well on its way to the boundary. The bottom hand comes into play more than in any other front-foot drive.

One to watch: Graeme Hick (England).

Advancing to drive requires nimble footwork and a lot of confidence. Try to move smoothly, and get into a firm position for the stroke.

And remember: if you do not reach the pitch of the ball to drive, you can always pull out of the shot, and play the ball

This lofted straight drive comes from my half-century on my Test debut against New Zealand at Old Trafford in 1994.

defensively. Far better that than to allow yourself to be stumped having a wild swing.

There is always an element of kidology between batsman and bowler when a batsman threatens to go down the wicket. The bowler should be alert to the slightest warning sign. The batsman can often feign to go down the wicket in the hope that the bowler responds by pitching the ball too short.

One to watch: Mark Waugh (Australia).

THE LEG GLANCE

When: The leg glance is a deflection off or outside the body which sends the ball down to fine leg. It can be played as a front-foot or a back-foot shot.

How: When glancing off the front foot, it is important to get your front foot inside the line of the ball – that is, between the ball and the stumps. Turn the face of the bat at the point of impact.

When glancing off the back foot, you will need to open your stance a little. Again, turn the bat at the point of impact. Don't go searching for the ball – let it come to you.

One to watch: Michael Atherton (England).

THE SWEEP

When: The only approved cross-batted shot played off the front foot, although quite a few unapproved ones pop up from time to time! Traditionally played to a slightly overpitched ball from a spin bowler, pitching outside leg-stump. Increasingly, though, many modern players are willing to sweep balls on the stumps, especially when the ball is not turning particularly sharply. In this case, they sweep more on length than line. Particularly risky if the ball is turning away from the bat.

How: To sweep successfully, your front foot should be on the line of the ball. Strike the ball in a sweeping motion from offside to legside. Bend the front leg fully, with the back leg trailing and make contact with the ball just after it pitches. By the time you play the shot, your bottom hand will be in control. Unless you are supremely strong – or the boundaries are very short – aim to hit the ball down. Roll the wrists and don't try to hit the ball too hard.

In recent years, the reverse sweep has gradually gained respectability. Its great beauty is that it disrupts a side's field positions, by sending the ball into unguarded areas. In one-day cricket, it particularly unsettles off-spinners bowling defensively to a packed legside field.

For **the reverse sweep**, the right-handed batsman must change his grip to that of a left-hander (and vice versa). It demands a keen eye and daredevil approach. Get out to a reverse sweep and prepare for criticism to rain down!

One to watch: Dermot Reeve (England).

Fig. 11: The sweep

THE SQUARE CUT

When: Played against a short ball, well wide of off-stump. If the ball is too close to the stumps, the shot will be cramped and the main danger is that you will chop the ball on to your stumps off the bottom edge. If the ball is too wide, you may overstretch and toe-end a catch, or not reach the ball at all.

How: This is basically a horizontal-bat shot, although it is safest to come down on the ball from above, as if you are chopping into a tree at waist level. Move your back foot back and across to around off-stump, and transfer your weight to your back foot. Upon playing the shot, your head should be above your back knee, which should be bent slightly. Another bottom-hand shot, where control is paramount.

A close relative of the square cut is **the late cut**. The intention is to play the ball along the ground in between the wicketkeeper and gully. Not a shot to play while a slip is still in residence! Your back shoulder and leg should point towards third man, in the direction of the shot. Let the ball pass your body so that it is almost alongside the stumps before you hit it. Steer the ball with a downward flick of the bat. Like the reverse sweep, another shot designed to unsettle a slow bowler's thinking.

One to watch: Robin Smith (England).

Fig. 12: The square cut

Fig. 13: The pull

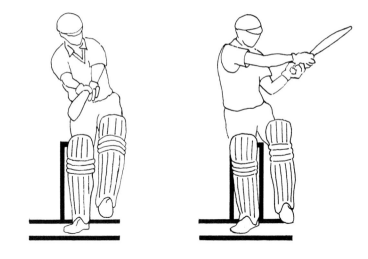

THE PULL

When: The pull shot is an attacking shot played against a long-hop which pitches on or around the stumps, and rises no higher than a batsman's stomach. It deposits the ball on the legside, generally between mid-on and square leg.

How: A cross-batted shot played with a lot of bottom hand.

Move your rear foot back and across to the offside, preferably outside the line of the ball. Your front foot swings round to the legside to open up your stance and point in the direction of the stroke. Straighten your arms and swing the bat horizontally in front of the body.

To keep the ball on the ground, angle the bat downwards. As you play the shot, your weight transfers from back to front foot, so bringing extra power. If you fail to switch your weight to the front foot, you will fall away and risk a half-hit shot straight up in the air.

One to watch: Graeme Hick (England).

THE HOOK

When: The hook shot combats a short ball or bouncer from a fast or fast-medium bowler which reaches the batsman between chest and head height. It aims to send the ball between square leg and fine leg, and is best played when the ball pitches on or outside leg stump. Like the pull, it is a cross-bat shot which

Fig. 14: The hook

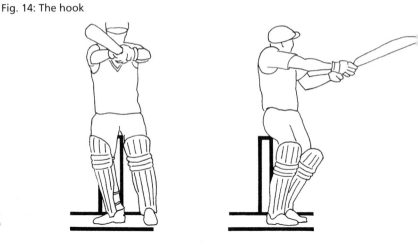

demands a quick eye and quick footwork. The hook will never be entirely safe, even for the finest player in the world. But against a top fast bowler, there is no more courageous or exciting shot in the game.

How: Open up your body and get your head fractionally outside the line of the ball – rapidly! Keeping your eyes on the ball is particularly important for this shot as a failure to do so could result in physical injury. Instinctively you will want to duck away, but if you cannot curb that movement, then do not play the shot.

Transfer your weight on to your back foot which acts as a pivot for the shot. Make contact at arm's length, on the legside of your body, hit through the ball and roll your wrists to keep the ball down. Your front foot swings in a semi-circle to finish pointing towards square leg.

One to watch: Alec Stewart (England).

TAKING EVASIVE ACTION

Vitally important for young players is to learn how to duck under or sway away from the quick short-pitched ball.

The TV pundit, and great former Yorkshire and England batsman, Geoffrey Boycott, advises that judgement of the line of a bouncer is vital when taking evasive action. During his career, if he met an offside bouncer, he would sway backwards; if it was straight or down the legside, he would duck underneath it. The vital thing is not to freeze, and never take your eye off the ball.

Allan Donald's bouncer did not hit me, so I must have been doing something right! A hair-raising moment during the 1994 Test series against South Africa.

The hook demands great practice – initially with a soft ball – and considerable ability. If you cannot play it with total conviction, do not play it at all.

One to watch: Mark Ramprakash (England).

BOWLING TIPS

The Run-up

Developing a reliable run-up is crucial. Even at Test level, bowlers continually encounter problems. During the series against the West Indies last summer, I dabbled with a longer run suggested by the former West Indies fast bowler, Michael Holding, but abandoned it by the end of the summer.

All bowlers' run-ups vary, but all of them need to follow basic guidelines to achieve success.

It is essential that the run-up enables a bowler to reach his delivery stride well balanced and at sufficient speed for the type of ball he intends to deliver.

A good run-up increases a fast bowler's pace and a slow bowler's ability to spin the ball. A consistent approach to the wicket also helps a bowler's accuracy, with the bowler's natural rhythm allowing him to settle into a reliable line and length.

You should aim to accelerate gradually, while maintaining a good rhythm. The more economical your action, the longer spells you will be able to bowl without getting tired. When marking out your run, you may wish to use two markers: one at the beginning of the run and one where you begin to pick up speed.

Practise your run-up until it feels like second nature.

One to watch: Craig McDermott (Australia).

The Delivery Stride and Basic Action

I'm a great believer in not interfering too much with a bowler's natural action. The orthodox side-on action is obviously an advantage, but many players have graduated to Test level with more square-on actions that have traditionally been frowned on by the coaches. If it works, don't fix it. But if it doesn't, then obviously the bowler needs to listen to some good advice.

Changing a bowler's action might bring vast improvements, but if done wrongly it might also arrest his development. It might remove flaws that would otherwise have caused him serious injury, but equally it might cause injury by asking the body to do something unnatural. Fine-tuning an action is fine, but it takes a top-class coach to consider whether a major restructuring operation is necessary.

The fact that I land on the side of my front foot in my delivery stride was held to have been a factor in my stress fracture on the last Ashes tour. Peter Lever, England's bowling coach, with the physio Wayne Morton looking on, has tried to get my entire foot to take the impact. I've even taken the chance to discuss with Peter the bowling advice in the following pages.

Basic advice is as follows:

- The penultimate stride in your bowling action must be the longest and fastest. When it is completed, take off from your left foot (assuming you are a right-arm bowler). Bound into your delivery stride, jumping high into a side-on action and rocking back.
- You move into your delivery stride as you land on your back foot (the right foot if you are a right-arm bowler). Your body twists into a side-on position.
- Take a final sideways step towards the crease, with your front hip and leg pointing down the pitch, and your back leg parallel to the crease. Keep your head upright and still.

My own delivery stride captured during the 1995 Test series against the West Indies. Check how many of the basic rules I have followed.

- Your front arm is thrown high towards the batsman. Look over your front shoulder, at the spot where you intend to pitch the ball.
- Bring your front arm down quickly, so dragging your bowling arm over.
- As you bring your front arm down, the bowling arm is extended behind the body. It then comes over quickly, high and straight behind your head.
- Exactly when the ball is released, and the exact operation of the wrist, depends upon what style of bowler you are.
- Follow through positively.

One to watch: Dominic Cork (England).

The Wrist Action

Never underestimate the importance of a good wrist action. Among club cricketers, it is probably the most unrecognised bowling skill, and yet it is absolutely essential for success.

One of the greatest assets of Australia's fast bowler, Craig McDermott, is his strong and stable wrist position. Wasim Akram, the Pakistani fast bowler, achieves much of his brilliance from his sleight of wrist. For Australia's leg-spinner, Shane Warne, of course, the wrist is paramount in his combination of leggies, googlies, top-spinners, flippers and invented mystery balls!

It is time for a simple explanation of the techniques involved in bowling certain deliveries.

Fast Bowling

Description: Fast bowlers defeat a batsman largely through sheer pace and bounce. If this is allied to movement in the air or off the pitch, they can be potentially devastating.

Ideal conditions: A fast pitch. Hard, bouncy pitches are sadly uncommon in England these days. The Oval is England's fastest pitch, while Perth (Australia) shares a reputation with several West Indies and South African wickets as among the quickest in the world. Wickets in Asia and New Zealand tend to be slow.

Method: Fast bowlers have a precious asset – pace. They are also highly individual, possessing a far greater variety of styles than your run-of-the-mill seam bowler. Any attempt to refine their technique must never threaten their natural pace.

That said, a fast bowler possessing a textbook action is fortunate indeed. As well as promising him greater control, he should also suffer less physical strain, and therefore stay freer from serious injury as a result. The basic action and techniques are the ideal for fast bowling.

For the out-and-out fast bowler, the run-up must be aggressive, and the delivery stride controlled but explosive. The bowling arm is a blur and the follow-through dynamic. Everything is geared to propelling the ball at speed.

True fast bowlers tend to be born, not made. But the greatest have shown a marvellous ability to learn the art as their career develops. Great fast bowlers such as Dennis Lillee, Malcolm Marshall, Richard Hadlee and Imran Khan all began as out-and-out quicks. By the end of their careers, their pace might have lessened, but they were accepted masters of their craft. The techniques outlined below were part of their armoury.

One to watch: Allan Donald (South Africa).

OUTSWINGERS

Description: An outswinger is a delivery, between medium-paced and fast, which moves in the air from the legside to the offside, i.e. away from the batsman. Late swing is much more dangerous.

Ideal conditions: A new ball, because of its greater shine and

Fig.15A and B: Outswinger grip.

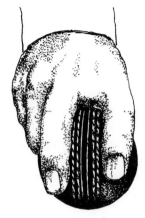 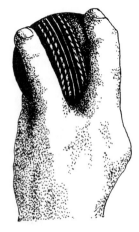

more prominent seam; a humid, overcast morning; and a breeze blowing across the ground from mid-on or fine leg.

Swing bowlers are always intent on keeping the shine on one side of the ball for as long as possible. A lush English outfield will protect the shine for much longer than a hard, dry ground experienced, for example, on the Indian sub-continent, where the shine can disappear remarkably quickly. Fielders who treat a new ball lazily, and allow it to roll or bounce back to the wicketkeeper, are giving the bowler no encouragement at all.

Method: Hold the ball with the seam running vertically, pointing towards first slip. Place your index and second fingers on either side of the seam, with the side of your thumb on the seam at the bottom. Hold the ball high in the hand, by the top joints of the fingers and thumb. Third and fourth fingers tuck down the side of the ball.

At the moment of release, steer the seam towards first slip. Place the shiny side of the ball on the legside – i.e. away from the chosen route of swing.

The basic action – which tends to drag the ball from leg to off – is ideal for bowling the outswinger.

(Mirror image: a left-handed bowler following this method would bowl an inswinger.)

One to watch: Dominic Cork (England).

INSWINGERS

Description: An inswinger is a delivery, between medium pace and fast, which moves in the air from the offside to the legside, i.e. into the batsman. Again, late swing possesses the most danger.

Ideal conditions: As for the outswinger, perfect conditions include a new ball and a humid, overcast day. In this case, though, the breeze is better coming from mid-off or third man.

Method: Hold the ball with the seam running vertically, pointing towards fine leg. Place your index finger slightly across the seam, with the second finger on top of it. The ball of your thumb rests on the seam underneath. Hold the ball high in the hand, by the top joints of the fingers. Tuck your third and fourth fingers down the side of the ball.

At the moment of release steer the seam towards fine leg. Place the shiny side of the ball on the offside – i.e. away from the chosen route of swing.

Fig. 16A and B:
Inswinger grip.

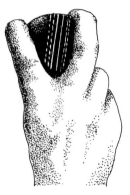

The action for the inswinger should be more open chested, with the ball pushed towards the off-stump. In an open-chested action, the bowler's back foot is more likely to be pointing in the direction of mid-on rather than parallel to the crease. The front foot would also be expected to move towards the batsman's off-stump rather than fine leg as in the basic action. A less arduous style than the outswinger – one to think about in middle age!

(Mirror image: a left-handed bowler following this method would bowl an outswinger.)

One to watch: Darren Gough (England).

REVERSE SWING

Description: The greatest, and most controversial, bowling development of recent years. Predominantly an inswinger, which swings late, although it can also be an outswinger.

Ideal conditions: A roughened old ball, devoid of shine, and often more than fifty overs old. One side is heavily scuffed, by such natural causes as a battering against the boundary boards or concrete, or a harsh, grassless pitch. Gamesmanship is not essential to reverse swing, although illegal ball-tampering can quicken the process. The other side of the ball (formerly the shiny side) is wetted.

Method: Because the wetter side of the ball is heavier than the scuffed side, it drags the ball down and an inswinger results. Known as reverse swing because many batsmen are conditioned, either by their experience earlier in the innings or by a bowler's action, to expecting an outswinger.

127

Explaining some of the basics of bowling to some willing students during my return to Priory School.

Reverse swing is still an inexact science – I bowl my reverse swing with an outswing action; Waqar Younis uses an inswing action. Reverse swing has been obtained primarily by skiddy bowlers with fast arm actions. At a speed under around seventy mph, it occurs very rarely, if at all, which does not make it an option for the average club player.

One to watch: Wasim Akram (Pakistan).

SEAM BOWLING

Description: A delivery which relies upon movement off the seam, when it hits the pitch, rather than in the air. It is also possible for swinging balls to seam even further off the pitch.

Ideal conditions: A ball with a prominent seam. A 'green' pitch – i.e. well grassed and damp – which is soft enough to allow the seam to bite upon landing. The seam is routinely cleaned. 'Picking' the seam, to make it sharper or more prominent, is illegal. Recent changes in regulations in English county cricket – a less prominent seam and firmer, dryer pitches – have aimed to make life harder for the traditional English seamer. But cricket at club level still offers them a potential field day.

Method: A good seamer relies heavily upon accuracy, subtlety and a shrewd knowledge of the game. The slower he is, the more controlled and intelligent his bowling must be.

The ball is basically held vertically down the seam, with slight variations in wrist position depending whether the ball is intended to seam away from or into the batsman. The two top fingers – the index finger and second finger – tend to be dragged back a little upon release. Good seamers expect to hit the seam almost without exception.

One to watch: Angus Fraser (England).

OFF-CUTTERS

Description: A delivery, between medium pace and medium-fast, which cuts back after pitching from off to leg. Occasionally curls away from the bat to begin with, which makes it a perfect alternative for an outswing bowler.

Ideal conditions: A wet pitch, or one which is dry and crumbling. Both encourage the ball to deviate. A breeze blowing from the legside encourages the ball to swing away before cutting back in the other direction. But regularly bowled under sufferance with old balls on slow, dead pitches when no one else fancies a bowl!

Method: The traditional grip resembles a conventional off-spinner, or finger spinner. Grip the ball firmly across the seam with the top joints of your thumb and first three fingers. At the moment of release, point the seam between cover and backward square leg. Drag your index and second fingers sharply down the outside of the ball, as if turning a door knob. Basic side-on action.

Alternatively, many bowlers use a basic outswinger's grip, but with the first finger wedged alongside the seam. This is more haphazard, but arguably has a greater surprise element.

(Mirror image: a left-arm bowler following this method would bowl a leg-cutter. The seam would point between midwicket and backward point.)

One to watch: Darren Gough (England).

Fig. 17: Off-cutter grip.

LEG-CUTTERS

Description: The leg-cutter is a delivery, between medium pace and medium-fast, which cuts after pitching from leg to off. Sometimes curls into the bat to begin with, which makes it a perfect alternative for an inswing bowler.

Ideal conditions: As the off-cutter, best bowled on a wet pitch, or one which is dry and crumbling. Both encourage the ball to deviate.

Method: The traditional grip resembles a conventional leg-spinner. Grip the ball firmly across the seam with the first three fingers and the thumb, evenly spaced. Index and second fingers should be on top of the ball. At the moment of release, point the seam between midwicket and backward point. The wrist then drags the index, second and third fingers sharply down the inside of the ball. Adopt the inswinger's chest-on action.

Alternatively, many bowlers use a basic inswinger's grip, but with the middle finger wedged against the seam. This is more haphazard, but arguably has a greater surprise element.

(Mirror image: a left-arm bowler following this method would bowl an off-cutter. The seam would point between cover and backward square leg.)

One to watch: Courtney Walsh (West Indies).

Fig. 18: Leg-cutter grip.

OFF-SPINNERS

Description: This delivery, bowled by a slow bowler, turns from the offside to the legside to a right-handed batsman. Traditionally, one of the most nagging styles of bowling.

Ideal conditions: A wearing pitch, which may be dusty or cracked, with the additional benefit of bowlers' footholds to bowl into. Alternatively a wet and drying wicket – if the seamers ever let go of the ball! Both offer the prospect of quick turn. A breeze blowing from the legside helps the off-spinner's outswinger. A headwind assists flight by making the ball drop suddenly in the air.

Method: The first finger is the chief spinning finger. It lies across the seam, with the top joint slightly bent and biting into the near edge of the seam. The second finger is stretched a wide but comfortable distance away, with the top joint again lying

Fig. 19A and B:
Off-spinner
grip.

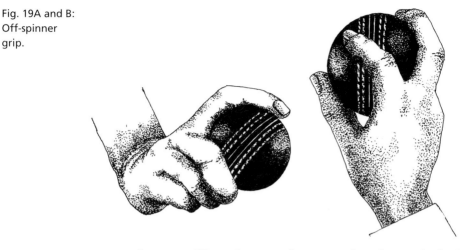

across the seam. The other two fingers curl underneath the ball, with the thumb resting on the other side, close to the seam.

The ball is spun by rotating the hand clockwise down the outside of the ball, much as turning a door knob. Don't be afraid to squeeze the ball.

The basic side-on body action suits the off-spinner. The bowler stands tall, delivering the ball across a braced front leg, and pivoting on the front foot. In the follow-through, the bowling arm whips across the body past the left hip.

The 'arm ball' offers important variation. It curves away, like an outswinger, towards the slips, and is especially useful if a batsman is persistently striking the turning off-spinner through the legside.

The seam is pointed towards the slips and the index and second finger grip loosely around the seam – not on it. At the moment of release, do not spin the ball, but steer the upright seam towards the slips.

Spin bowlers tend to stress more than anyone the importance of bowling a good sequence of deliveries. Cricket is a mind game, and efforts to lull a batsman into a mistake can take several overs.

(Mirror image: a left-arm bowler following the off-spinner's method becomes a conventional left-arm spinner, turning the ball away from the right-hander. His arm ball drifts into the right-handed batsman.)

One to watch: old videos of John Emburey (England)!

LEG-SPINNERS
Description: Leg-spin, bowled by a slow bowler, turns the ball

from leg to off, by a flicking of the wrist on delivery. Wrist-spin is an immensely challenging and exciting art, but to anyone who masters it, the rewards can be boundless.

Other forms of wrist spin include:

- **The googly:** spins the opposite way from off to leg.
- **The top-spinner:** tends to fall steeper and bounce more.
- **The flipper:** hurries low on to the batsman at high speed.

Ideal conditions: A good wrist-spinner can turn the ball on the most unhelpful surface. A wearing or sticky pitch is an obvious advantage, but a wicket possessing pace and bounce can be equally encouraging. A breeze, preferably from fine leg, can also add to a batsman's uncertainty.

Method: To bowl the leg-spinner, hold the ball firmly in the first three fingers and base of the thumb. The seam lies across the joint of the first two fingers, with the bent third finger lying across the seam. The first and third fingers should be stretched and squeezed tightly.

At the moment of delivery, the seam is angled between midwicket and gully. The wrist is cocked inwards. As the ball is released, the wrist flips the fingers forward anticlockwise. The third finger, which drags across the seam towards gully, is the chief spinning finger.

Few leg-spinners maintain the same levels of accuracy as other styles of bowlers although Australia's Shane Warne is a

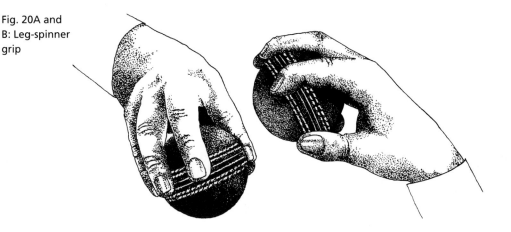

Fig. 20A and B: Leg-spinner grip

shining exception. That is why they must develop other deliveries to outwit and bamboozle a batsman, notably the googly, top-spinner and flipper. All need ceaseless practice to bowl; only the best ever perfect them.

The googly – or wrong 'un – is an off-break bowled with what looks deceptively like leg-break action. The basic grip is the same, but the difference occurs in the wrist action. The ball must be delivered out of the back of the hand. At the moment of release, push your third finger towards square leg rather than gully, so imparting the spin.

The top-spinner does not spin, but defeats a batsman in the flight, looping shorter and bouncing higher than anticipated. Particularly effective against a batsman fond of the drive. At the moment of release, the third finger is pushed forwards over the top of the ball so that the seam rotates in a straight line towards the batsman.

The flipper also turns little, if at all, but hurries low on to an unsuspecting batsman. Particularly effective against a batsman who likes to pull and cut. The basic intention is to impart back-spin. While the body, arm and hand are moving forward, the fingers (particularly the first finger) snap back in the opposite direction. Exceptionally difficult to bowl.

Wrist-spin, in all its forms, is the most difficult bowling skill of all. If you can master all these deliveries, you are well on the way to a fulfilling Test career!

(Mirror image: the left-arm wrist spinner (a rare species found largely in Australia) is referred to as a chinaman bowler.)

One to watch: Shane Warne (Australia).

FIELDING AND WICKETKEEPING

No aspect of cricket has improved as much in the past twenty years as fielding. Whereas once it was easy to hide immobile players in the field, nowadays virtually every position has its own special demands.

In chapter six, Graeme Hick and Graham Thorpe gave their own advice on close catching and outfielding. Fielding in the *inner ring* is equally important. Positions such as cover and midwicket often are patrolled by the slickest fielders in the side. A world-class cover fielder such as South Africa's Jonty Rhodes will grab attention by the occasional brilliant catch, stop or run-out. But all the time he is inhibiting the batsman by his presence, adding to the uncertainty which the bowler is striving to create.

Wasim Akram, Pakistan's captain, is adamant that fielding is the area of cricket where practice can do most to turn mediocrity into excellence. Your youth and agility might give you an

Providing slip catching practice before Yorkshire's NatWest first round tie against Devon at Exmouth in 1994.

advantage over older players and be enough for you to pull off some excellent moments. But practice will bring greater consistency and even more outstanding moments. Don't regard fielding practice as a bind – it's important to get your reactions in shape before the game begins.

Fig. 21: Fielding positions.

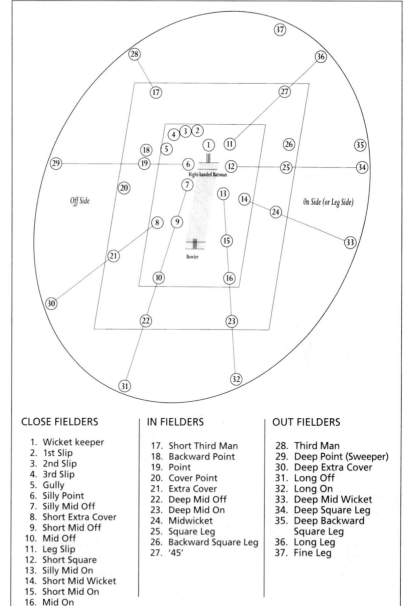

CLOSE FIELDERS

1. Wicket keeper
2. 1st Slip
3. 2nd Slip
4. 3rd Slip
5. Gully
6. Silly Point
7. Silly Mid Off
8. Short Extra Cover
9. Short Mid Off
10. Mid Off
11. Leg Slip
12. Short Square
13. Silly Mid On
14. Short Mid Wicket
15. Short Mid On
16. Mid On

IN FIELDERS

17. Short Third Man
18. Backward Point
19. Point
20. Cover Point
21. Extra Cover
22. Deep Mid Off
23. Deep Mid On
24. Midwicket
25. Square Leg
26. Backward Square Leg
27. '45'

OUT FIELDERS

28. Third Man
29. Deep Point (Sweeper)
30. Deep Extra Cover
31. Long Off
32. Long On
33. Deep Mid Wicket
34. Deep Square Leg
35. Deep Backward
    Square Leg
36. Long Leg
37. Fine Leg

Wicketkeeping has changed in character as well. A general move to seam-orientated attacks, and one-day cricket has reduced the amount of opportunity that wicketkeepers have to stand up to the wicket. But it is here that great wicketkeepers often make their mark, and any budding 'keepers should put special emphasis on this area of their game.

Most important in a wicketkeeper's stance is that it should be well balanced, with the weight comfortably distributed between both feet. Quick leg movement is essential, and training should concentrate on strengthening your leg muscles. All that crouching can be tiring work!

When standing back, aim to take the ball at the point where it is just beginning to fall, around waist height. Many novice 'keepers make the mistake of standing too far back to give themselves more time and end up groping for the ball around their ankles. Position yourself wide of the off-stump so that you can see the ball all the way from the bowler's hand. Anticipate the line of the ball as early as possible.

When standing up, imagine a semi-circle behind the stumps and make this your working area. Always ensure that you are close enough to the stumps to be able to pull off a stumping.

Medium-pace bowlers might leave you undecided whether to stand up or stand back. Stand up if you want to restrict a batsman, and dissuade him from moving out of his crease, or if you fancy a stumping is on the cards. Stand back if your priority is a less high-risk approach, with the emphasis upon saving runs and taking the straightforward catches.

To reduce the risk of injury, never point your fingers towards the ball. To reduce the jarring on your hands, give with the ball as it comes into your hands. Never snatch. Do not rise from your stance too early. Concentrate, and assume even on the flattest deck that every ball is coming your way.

A tidy wicketkeeper can have a positive effect on the rest of the side, whereas a bad 'keeper can set in motion a dreadful fielding performance.

Always be alert to the possibility of a run-out. It's your responsibility to be up to the stumps whenever necessary. Chivvy your fielders into backing-up at all times and into providing you with accurate returns. Encourage the bowler – you are in the best position to advise him on possible tactics.

10 Brave New World

Floodlit county cricket on the top six grounds in the country. That is just one way that I would transform the game and bring fresh excitement to a new generation of supporters.

The fuddy-duddys will fling their sandwich boxes down in protest, but I'm making no apologies. Cricket must strive harder to attract a younger audience if it is not to be overtaken by other sports more willing to grasp the future with both hands. Satellite TV, with its specialist sports channels, offers untold opportunities, but only those sports keenly aware of the audience's wishes will fully benefit.

I'm familiar with all the tired reasons lined up against floodlit cricket. Opponents will argue that it is simply too expensive, that floodlight pylons will disfigure the grounds, that England is just too cold. They will point to the financial disaster of the floodlit event at The Oval at the end of the 1994 season and claim that it proves there is no demand.

With pessimism like this, England would still be a desert island with everybody still playing their favourite gramophone records on clapped-out machines.

I played in a few floodlit exhibition games at the Don Valley stadium in Sheffield a couple of years ago. We played on a matting wicket draped in the middle of a rugby outfield. Far from ideal. In fact, it was about as far away from the real thing as you could get. But 17,000 spectators turned out on a rainy night to watch Yorkshire play a World XI. Interest in a properly contested day-night competition between recognisable first-class counties on Test grounds would be much easier to sustain.

Under my plan, three counties would play head-to-head matches at each Test ground, with the six group winners qualifying for the semi-finals. These would consist of two more groups of three, with the winners in each semi-final group playing a best-of-three final.

Start a one-day match at five o'clock, between mid-June and the end of August, and the younger spectators would come

It's time that English cricket administrators recognised the attractions of day-night cricket with a new floodlit county competition. I'll never forget the atmosphere during the last match of my Ashes tour, against Australia in Melbourne.

flocking in. It would be a chance for an evening out, something to do after a hard day at school or at work. It wouldn't be all that cold, either – 20-over evening leagues have prospered in England for years.

There is more money than ever in the game since the Test and County Cricket Board's £60 million TV deal. Some of it should be invested in providing floodlights for all six Test grounds, including Lord's.

Many MCC members will splutter that the character of Lord's would be irreparably damaged. But there is no more traditionally beautiful ground in the world than the Adelaide Oval and they have managed to find a tasteful and imaginative solution, by opting for retractable floodlights. If one of our Test grounds does not feel up to the task, then a go-ahead county like Durham, or perhaps Hampshire if their new ground at Southampton comes to fruition, should be offered the chance to take their place.

I have loved nothing better in my England career than the chance to play a day-night international in front of an excitable, capacity crowd. The atmosphere is extraordinary with the lights blazing, everybody cheering and people enjoying a few beers.

In Australia last winter, we played a day-night international in front of thirty-odd thousand in Sydney, followed that by a run-of-the-mill daytime match in Brisbane, when the ground was less than half full, and it was a matter of just getting the game over with, and then had another day-nighter in Melbourne in front of 70,000. Fantastic. I would like to play in one of those games every week.

The more elderly cricket followers who are appalled by such ideas would still find more than enough traditional Test and championship cricket to keep them happy. But insisting that traditions never change is plain selfish, and risks damaging the game they profess to love. Youth must have its say, and if younger supporters want to sing and chant in support of their team, then I for one will thank them for it.

I've been staggered by the amount of criticism heaped upon the Barmy Army during England's last two overseas tours. England have always been followed by a few well-heeled supporters with the money to follow their dreams. But the supporters who made up the Barmy Army included everybody from solicitors to dustbinmen, all travelling halfway round the world to support England. Some of these spectators gave up jobs, many of them backpacked their way around Australia and South Africa and stayed in the cheapest accommodation that they could find. They didn't just go to get drunk and have a good time. Only once, after a day's play at Sydney, can I remember a couple of them getting abusive.

When we made a late surge in the Christmas Test at Sydney in 1994, but did not quite achieve victory, they sang 'we're proud of you' for more than an hour after the match. No disrespect to the older spectators – we need them too – but to hear somebody young chanting your name is a personal connection that makes you swell with pride.

Nearly all the England team were happy to socialise with them at the end of the tour and thank them for their support. And yes, it is true, we also handed down an occasional can of Tetley bitter from dressing room balconies to keep their throats well lubricated. No one expects to go to a top football match and hear ninety minutes of polite clapping; the atmosphere is part of the thrill.

To those who say cricket comes from a different tradition, then I say it's time those traditions were changed.

I'd have music playing during drinks intervals, and adverts

on the big screens. On the England A tour to South Africa in 1994, they played jingles at some matches whenever a batsman hit a four. Good for them, let's have more of it. And when batsmen walk out to the wicket, what's wrong with a big introduction – a few bars of music, followed by the player's name? It is all about presentation. Instead, the announcement is solemn, dull, boring. At some county matches, the announcer is wheezing so much, you don't know whether to walk out to bat or rush off and call an ambulance.

Another idea that should be adopted in Test and county cricket is names and numbers on players' clothing. Shirt names have already come to pass in the AXA Equity & Law Sunday League, and no one can argue that identification is not much easier. I'm not proposing coloured clothing in all competitions – whites are here to stay, as far as I'm concerned – but there would be nothing distasteful in a name on the back of a shirt, or a modestly sized number beneath the sponsor's logo on the arm or the trouser pocket. In the days of helmets, quick and easy identification is all important. A few spectators might take pride in their ability to identify all twenty-two players in a county match, but we are not running a spot-the-player contest. Casual spectators, perhaps wandering into their first match for a couple of years, deserve to know what is going on.

I'm not suggesting that cricket should become a two-bit circus, not for a moment. I'm a staunch supporter of the move to four-day championship cricket, which on modern pitches is a far more worthwhile game than the three-day version which preceded it. Four-day cricket demands more commitment from the county player, and a greater awareness from the paying public. At its best, command of a four-day match has to be earned, often over several days, on a pitch that demands excellence from both batsmen and bowlers alike. By contrast, three-day cricket was either a keen contest on an inferior pitch, which did little to develop Test cricketers, or a con to the paying public, with players largely going through the motions on a flat surface for the first seven sessions, before manufacturing a run-chase on the final afternoon. The only mistake has been to insert a Sunday League match in the middle of the four-day game. That disastrously interrupts the flow of the most prestigious county competition. After a hard-fought Sunday League game, my Monday mornings are a nightmare. If you are lucky, you wake up exhausted. Unlucky, and you wake up injured.

It used to infuriate me when I looked in the paper at the averages and saw limited players with fifty or sixty first-class wickets. All right, they were good enough to play county cricket, but their rewards were often out of proportion with their talents. Four-day cricket divides the best players from the run-of-the-mill players, because it gives the batters longer to bat and makes the bowlers bowl players out.

It was amazing in three-day cricket how many bowlers were given cheap wickets by slogs or lazy shots. Any bowler who had been around for a while sensed when a declaration was approaching, and would suddenly be eager for another bowl to touch up their figures.

Batting averages could also be distorted. At Yorkshire, the dressing room used to joke how often Phil Robinson would be batting when the 'deccie' bowlers came on, but it's amazing how often it used to happen. Nowadays, when cheap runs are being tossed up, some counties have the pride to send their lower-order batsmen in to bat; that's how it should be.

The greater commitment demanded in four-day cricket should be reflected by other decisions to make the championship more competitive. I'd have no qualms about two divisions of nine teams, with automatic promotion and relegation. That would create far more interest in the media, and down at the local pub, and the more that people are talking about the game, the healthier its future will be. We should announce that a two-division system will operate from the year 2000 and that results in the three seasons between 1997 and 1999 will determine in which division each county will play. In the first division, certainly, I would play only eight four-day matches a season. That would ensure that players prepared more seriously for each game, and entered it in the peak physical and mental condition.

If Michael Bevan, Yorkshire's overseas batsman, fails in a couple of Sheffield Shield matches for New South Wales, then he knows his place is in jeopardy. Success and failure would become far more important, and we would rid the championship of the attitude that another chance is always just around the corner. Seventeen four-day matches breeds stale and exhausted players at best, injured players at worst.

Pitches have also got to be quicker and flatter. I know it sounds funny, coming from a bowler, but I hate bowling on surfaces that seam around viciously. It might be because of the

Quick pitches encourage daring cricket from batsmen and bowlers alike.

type of bowler I am, relying more on pace and bounce than movement, but there is more to cricket than just running up on slow pitches and dropping the ball on the spot. But, look at the Whyte & Mackay ratings and the top ten is still dominated by traditional English seamers.

I'm not saying that I haven't got a lot to learn – I'll be learning until the day I retire or that Yorkshire sack me. And I know that I didn't cash in on the succession of damp, seaming pitches encountered by Yorkshire throughout May and June last year, when Peter Hartley outperformed me time and again. Peter had learned his craft over more than a decade and knew exactly how to adjust. Steve Watkin, at Glamorgan, and Tim Munton, at Warwickshire, are also highly skilled and valued performers.

But me, I still want to bowl fast, and that is the way I'm going to make the grade as a successful Test bowler. Maybe I'll be grateful for a slow seamer when I'm deep into my thirties, and my body is beginning to slow up, but at the moment I can live without them. Batsmen struggle along at two runs an over because the ball isn't coming on to the bat, so when bowlers of extra pace come on, like myself or Devon Malcolm, it can often make things easier for them. Give me a wicket with enough pace and even bounce for the ball to carry to the wicketkeeper and slips.

Even the pitches in Australia on England's 1994–5 tour were

a disappointment. After our first two games in Western Australia, at Lilac Hill and the WACA in Perth, I could hardly conceal my excitement. I thought, 'This is going to be one hell of a trip.' But as soon as we travelled east, we met a succession of tracks so sluggish, that we might as well have been playing in England.

In the Tests, everything was made to favour Shane Warne's leg-spin. That's not on. Test cricket is too important to be mucked about with. Quick pitches encourage daring cricket from batsmen and bowlers alike, and create a far better spectacle. And that is how it should be.

11 Telling Tales

I've come to accept that many people like to tell tall stories about me. Some of them are so exaggerated that I wonder if they are talking about the same bloke. But I don't mind keeping them happy, as long as it's all in good fun. So here is their opportunity, and don't blame me if it is all too unbelievable for words.

Wayne Morton
Yorkshire and England physiotherapist, and a source of great encouragement to me.

Here goes my favourite after-dinner story! During one of Yorkshire's pre-season tours to South Africa, Darren was persuaded by Paul Jarvis to visit a Cape Town guru. Jarv was blessed with a quicksilver tongue and managed to persuade Darren that the guru would be able to tell him what the future held.

Goughie was keen to try something different, so off they went, and soon the guru, a old black South African with short grey hair and a walking stick, got to work.

Goughie was quick to tell the guru that his ambitions were to become an England fast bowler. The guru contemplated this for a while, then said, 'At the end of your run, kiss the ball like this and recite the Lord's Prayer. Then you will bowl like the wind.'

Come the next match at Newlands, Darren was aching to put the theory into practice. Here was the secret that could change his entire career. He reached the end of his run, kissed the ball, and could be seen by his team-mates mumbling quietly to himself. Then he sprinted in, and bowled a rank long hop which was pulled out of the ground.

At the lunch interval, an obviously dischuffed Goughie was asked what had gone wrong. 'Well, it was all right until I got to the bit about the Lord's Prayer,' he said, 'but then I couldn't quite remember all of it, so I just made do with "For what we are about to receive."'

Dazzler's accuracy rating: eight out of ten. The punch line is

Wayne's invention, but otherwise it's pretty much a true story. The guru has since asked me for 'protection money', but I never got round to giving him any. He even claimed that he was responsible for my stress fracture in Australia. It makes you wonder.

Paul Grayson
Former Yorkshire all-rounder, now with Essex. Best man at Darren's wedding.

Funnily enough, we didn't get on well together at first. I think Goughie thought I was a North Yorkshire snob. I remember an occasion at the Uppingham Festival – for under-16 county sides – when I was getting a bit uppity and called him 'pit boy'. Pit bull was more like it as he took a massive swing at me. 'Call me pit boy again and I'll knock your block off,' he said. We've got on famously since then.

On his wedding day, I was intrigued to hear Darren doing his speech in an American accent. It was all accidental. He was speaking after his father-in-law, John, who is from the States, and was so nervous he just slipped into the American twang. During the service he also tried to put the ring on the wrong hand; the vicar had to sort that one out. It's all on the video.

I'm also a great fan of Goughie's conversational muddles. He is a big pasta eater now, but when he first started, he once asked at a lunch interval at Old Trafford for 'tagaletty'.

We had a fines box in the Yorkshire dressing room one season for anybody saying or doing anything daft – by the end of the season Goughie was skint. What can you say when someone walks into a dressing room one morning and announces that he has 'just seen a fella shave his head off for charity'?

Dazzler's accuracy rating: nine out of ten. The only thing wrong with this story is that I put the ring on the wrong hand. As far as I remember, I almost put my ring on Anna's finger!

Martyn Moxon
Yorkshire and England.

Remember the time two years ago when Chris Lewis posed nude in *For Women* magazine? All tasteful stuff, I'm told, but not an everyday occurrence for an England cricketer.

Well, in a quiet moment at Abbeydale Park one day, the Yorkshire dressing room decided to take things a little further. Darren was told that *GQ* magazine wanted him to model underwear. Big bucks were involved – money that would make Chris Lewis' payment seem like a couple of spare coppers.

Goughie's eyes popped out of his head. Should he do it? What would Yorkshire think? More to the point, what would Anna, his wife, think? We strung him along for half a day or more. I told him that the *GQ* researcher had promised to call back later in the day and that, in the meantime, it was essential that he asked Yorkshire for permission.

Steve Oldham, our director of cricket, was also in on the joke. He insisted that Goughie was banned from even discussing it. The whole affair finished with Chalkie White phoning Goughie in a woman's voice from a nearby telephone. By then, he began to suspect a wind-up. Afterwards, he blustered that he had always known that we were stringing him along, but we're not convinced.

Dazzler's accuracy rating: eight out of ten. OK, I was sucked in for the first hour, but then I realised it was a wind-up when I called GQ and asked if they knew the name of the reporter who was coming to see me. From then on, I just played along with it.

Ralph Middlebrook
Leeds City Council cricket development officer, and manager of Yorkshire Cricket School.

Stories about Goughie! Do you want me to fill the book? He came to the Headingley indoor school after Rotherham United had lost interest in him. He told the local job centre that he could play cricket, they phoned me to check if he had any potential, and he soon joined us on a Youth Training Scheme.

He was a big eater in those days, was Goughie. He used to go up to the Original Oak pub for his lunch with Steve Bethel, another of our lads. Under their food system, they sold you the meat, and the rest was self-service. Darren put so much food on his plate that he tripped up and it fell all over the floor. He insists he didn't eat it off the carpet.

Every day we clean the floor of the indoor school with a Rotorwash. It's not a very popular job, but it keeps one of the lads out of mischief for a while. In his second year with us, Darren managed to topple the machine over and water flooded all over the floor. He diligently cleaned up, but afterwards the machine wouldn't start. Darren's solution was to send one of the first-year trainees to a local garage for some petrol. Neither of them realised it ran on electricity.

His attitude to batting hasn't changed one bit – he still leans back and throws the bat at the ball. In his early days, I used to admire his outswinger and he used to be impressed with my leg-cutter. Things have changed a bit since then.

Dazzler's accuracy rating: seven out of ten. I certainly stuffed the first-year trainee. We had great fun as I sent him off for £4 worth of petrol. It got us all half an hour's rest.

Steve Rhodes
Worcestershire and England.

If nobody else is going to tell it, then I'll lay claim to the story about Goughie's unexpected captaincy ambitions on the England A tour to South Africa. Darren loves the limelight – things are never boring when he's around – but few of us ever suspected that the mysterious art of captaincy had ever entered his head.

Hugh Morris skippered England A in South Africa, and a happy and successful bunch we were, too. Hugh has a quiet sense of fun, so when Darren announced that he 'quite fancied this captaincy business', it was time for a spot of gentle leg-pulling.

'So what would you do then, Dazzler, if you were in charge tomorrow?' Hugh asked.

Darren gave the matter serious thought. 'Well,' he finally said, 'I reckon the lads have worked hard recently, and deserve some reward. As lots of girlfriends are out here at the moment, I'd give us all a day off and let us go down to the beach.'

We all get disorientated with the ceaseless travelling on tour, but Goughie was obviously more confused than most.

'Do you realise,' said Hugh, 'just how far Pretoria is away from the sea?'

Dazzler's accuracy rating: ten out of ten. I've never been very good at geography.

David Norrie
News of the World *cricket correspondent, and in that newspaper, the driving force behind Darren's Diary.*

Nobody has ever been in any doubt about Darren's gift for the outrageous and the extraordinary. I remember half-watching Sky TV's daily pitch report during England's tour of Australia. Just as Tony Greig was sticking his car keys into the pitch, or

Handstands
down under . . .
for the benefit
of Sky TV!

something, one morning, in the background there was Goughie, walking by on his hands. If Greig had seen him, he would have been so surprised that he would have fallen down one of the cracks.

Some of the dozier reporters are ready to believe anything about Darren. I made good use out of this with one particularly successful wind-up in Australia. Hours before the start of the first Test in Brisbane, Darren was awoken by a telephone call from his wife, Anna, to learn that she had given birth to their first son, Liam. It was a simple matter to suggest that Darren was so thrilled that he had vowed to christen his son with the middle names of any Australian batsman he managed to dismiss on the first day. One fanciful journalist (not a million miles away from the back flap of this book) watched Goughie dismiss Boon and Bevan by the close and proudly announced to his readers that 'Liam David Michael Gough was born'.

Darren occasionally struggles with the technical side of life. In Australia, he was having trouble with his CD Walkman, and he decided to go out and buy a new set of speakers. When he got them back to the hotel, he made quite a fuss about them not working, how he wouldn't have a chance to return them, and about all the money he had wasted. I didn't like to interrupt, but I thought it best to point out that he hadn't switched the power on.

I've never seen Darren more serious than the day I took him, and Graham Gooch, to meet Harold Larwood. When it comes to Ashes series, 'Lol' is the man. England have never produced a finer fast bowler, and his part in the Bodyline series in Australia in the early 1930s is legendary. I know that Darren was grateful to have the chance to meet him before his death last summer. During their chat, Darren asked Larwood, quite seriously, if he had ever pitched the ball up during the Bodyline series. 'No,' laughed Larwood, and looked at him as if he was joking. It must be the only time in his life that Goughie has been deadly serious, and nobody realised!

Dazzler's accuracy rating: ten out of ten. Enjoyed the handstand – Greigy saw it and thought it was great. Channel 9 used it before start of play.

Mark Ilott
Essex and England left-arm seamer, who was first a team-mate of mine at England under-19 level.

I see Paul Grayson has already told the one about 'Chicken Tagaletty'. What he didn't say was that, according to Darren, it came with Veal Esca-lopez, pronounced as in Nancy Lopez. Sorry, Darren, had to get that one in.

I can never remember all the others. You don't need to. Darren's funny remarks are like buses, you know there will be another one along in a minute. There was the story, though, on the England A tour of South Africa, about him wondering if he had got altitude sickness. We were in Durban at the time – slap bang at sea level. He will tell you whether it's true or not.

Dazzler's accuracy rating: five out of ten. Sorry, Ramble, but you've got a bad memory on the altitude sickness . . . it wasn't me! But I'll give you the Veal Esca-lopez . . . nearly!

Michael Henderson
Cricket writer, The Times

Darren began to emerge as an England player on the A tour to South Africa in 1993. From the moment that he took wickets against Western Province in Cape Town, he began to attract the attention of the media, including the BBC's urbane young cricket reporter, Simon Mann. One section of the resulting radio interview has become the stuff of A tour folklore.

'If I keep bowling like this,' said Darren, 'you never know.'

'You never know what, Darren?' enquired Mann, tongue in cheek.

'Well, you know,' said Darren. 'You just never know.'

Dazzler's accuracy rating: three out of ten. Did the interview, but can't remember the exact conversation. Have to mark this one the lowest of the lot.

Dave Roberts
Former England physiotherapist.

Far from me to want to take the mickey, but as you've asked me . . . Darren has always had a tremendous urge to do well at Headingley, but things have never quite worked out his way. The first Test against the West Indies in 1995 was a case in point. Early in the Test, before England began to run into trouble, Goughie was relaxing in the players' viewing area. After lunch, resting on his elbows, he began ruminating, addressing no one in particular but unable to stay silent for a moment longer.

'You know,' he said, gazing out at the Western Terrace, 'if I carry on doing well in this Test cricket lark, like I did in Australia, they might name that stand over there after me one day.'

Goughie seemed to forget that Yorkshire have never been quick to name stands after any of their great players. There was the Len Hutton Bar for a while, but before he died Sir Leonard, uncomfortable with a link with alcohol, asked for his name to be removed.

And it has to be said that, on this occasion, Goughie did not possess the art of perfect timing. Headingley has not been his lucky Test ground. Sure enough, a year after his two for plenty in the first innings against South Africa, he followed up against the West Indies by being out first ball and picking up a bowling injury during his second delivery of the game. Everything that could go wrong did so.

However much the Western Terrace cheered him, and however much beer had been consumed there, the idea of 'The Darren Gough Stand' had to be put back for a while.

Whenever he bowled badly for England after that, we were always quick to enquire which part of the ground they might name after him.

Darren is also one of the loudest golfers that I have ever played with or against. Before the 1994 Headingley Test, he was thrashing around the undergrowth at least two hundred yards behind the rest of the four-ball. We all assumed that he had given up the hole when suddenly, as I drew my putter back for a birdie putt, Darren's ball landed a foot behind me, to an accompanying holler – 'Tremendous, look at that, brilliant' – which must have been heard by everyone on the course. My putt missed; Darren, of course, sunk his for a birdie.

Dazzler's accuracy rating: ten out of ten. Rooster is always complaining because he's never beaten me at golf and probably never will.

Dave Roberts just tells tall stories about my golf because he knows he will never beat me! The secret is in how you bite the tee peg . . .

12 Dazzler's A to Z

A: Agents

. . . And, more specifically, Advantage International, the second largest sports management company in the world, who have represented me superbly since my return from England's tour of Australia. Some people asked, 'Why does Goughie need an agent?' and wondered if I was getting too big for my boots. In Yorkshire, they don't like you to act as if you are from the better side of the street.

But after my tour of Australia came to a premature end because of my foot injury, we were receiving up to forty telephone calls a day at home. The answerphone would fill up, wind back to the start and fill up again. Anna had recently given birth to Liam and we needed some family time together. It was all threatening to swamp us.

It was obvious that I was in big demand. Nobody knew whether such attention would last two minutes or ten years. But Advantage International, a United States company, who represent top stars such as the world number one women's tennis player, Steffi Graf, took a tremendous weight off me.

While I know that my financial affairs are being professionally looked after, I can concentrate on my cricket. I don't want to be negotiating my own equipment deals, or weighing up whether I should accept offers of personal appearances. Before I know it, I might skip a visit to the gym and that's where the trouble starts. And I'm not interested in linking my name to every product that comes my way, turning up to open new supermarkets, or doing anything where I can't be myself.

Agents are not exclusively about money. If I prefer to use one company's equipment, then that is the company I want to be involved with. Agents have a bad name in England, particularly in football, where there might well be a few chancers about, but I'm happy that Advantage International are playing a positive role in my career.

B: Bouncers

A courageous hook shot against a wickedly fast bouncer is one of the most exciting sights in cricket. But you hear all sorts of wild theories about curbing short-pitched bowling. One crackpot suggestion is that a white line should be drawn halfway down the pitch, and any ball pitched behind it should be classified as a no-ball. That is about as daft as the Americans who clamoured to make football goals wider during the last World Cup so that there would be more goals.

I believe we've got the balance exactly right in Test cricket. In fact, I'm in favour of the current Test regulations being extended to the rest of the first-class game: a maximum of two bouncers per over.

International umpires appealed last September for no restrictions at all. They wanted to be free to judge for themselves, and to rely upon the law that outlaws short-pitched fast bowling when umpires reckon there is a danger of physical injury to the batsman. In my opinion, the two limitations work well together – a combination of simple arithmetic and an umpire's gut feeling.

Bouncers come in various shapes and sizes. There is the skiddy type of bouncer, delivered by bowlers like myself and Paul Jarvis, those of us who will never quite be six feet tall unless platform shoes make an amazing comeback. Wasim Akram is a similar type, but being left-arm, he comes at a different angle, and causes me endless problems.

Then there are the bouncers bowled by people like Allan Donald, Devon Malcolm and most of the West Indians, Ian Bishop, Curtly Ambrose and Kenny Benjamin. The taller they are, the steeper the bounce. Donald's bouncer is the quickest in the world, but his action is so smooth that you can predict it better than some.

Another plus point when bowling bouncers is the surprise element. Dominic Cork and Craig White are both capable of bouncers that are far quicker than their stock ball, which can often catch batsmen unawares. Many bowlers also develop a slower and a faster bouncer. Batsmen congratulating themselves on hooking the former West Indian great, Michael Holding, for four would find the next ball fizzing rapidly past their nose. In this case, the first bouncer is often a set-up.

The bouncer that gives me most trouble of all is that of the West Indian, Courtney Walsh. He is a wise old bird, is

Courtney, and rarely bowls a short ball that does not need to be played. Everything is directed towards the body, and can rarely be avoided by a simple duck or sway of the head. Then courage and an instinct for self-preservation are vital.

Sadly, there are some pitches where it is futile trying to bowl a bouncer. At Scarborough last season, the pitch was so slow that the ball hardly got above stump high. For a fast bowler, that removes thirty per cent of your armoury. If I'd been batting against me, I'd have been thinking, 'What a piece of cake.' In those circumstances, don't waste your energy.

C: Crowds

If my middle stump went cartwheeling out of the ground in the middle of a Test, while the crowd were doing a Mexican wave, I wouldn't even hear it. Journalists might ask me a few hours later whether my concentration was affected, and some of them would probably write that crowd misbehaviour must be clamped down upon, but you will never hear such excuses from me.

One occasion when the mood of a crowd did contribute to my dismissal was on my home ground at Headingley last year, in the first Cornhill Test against the West Indies. And it was all my own fault.

In bad times and good, for the past six seasons, Yorkshire supporters had always urged me on. After my success in Australia, I was desperate to repay them, and when I walked out to bat, the noise was deafening. Because crowds chant and cheer more these days, I reckon I probably even beat Geoffrey Boycott's record decibel reading!

I was so pumped up that when Ian Bishop delivered the bouncer, the hook was automatic, and as much as 20,000 people bellowed, they could not quite shout it over the ropes at long leg. Another painful lesson.

I'm often asked to explain my rapport with crowds the world over. There is no big secret. If they ask me a question, I'll answer them. If they abuse me, I just try to make a joke of it. If they pull a face, I might pull one back. It all helps to pass the time in the field. If someone asks you for your autograph, you should also remember that it is a privilege. Sometimes when you are hot and sweaty, it all seems a trial, but the day will soon come when I won't even be recognised in my own street.

There are times, such as in the Edgbaston Test last year, when

The Barmy Army have attracted criticism for their vocal support of England overseas, but they will receive none from me – or from most England players.

I've been cheered to the rafters, even though I know I've been playing badly. It is a relationship that I value, and I hope that many of the spectators do too. Modern sportsmen have become increasingly cut off from their public, one drawback, I'm afraid, of greater financial reward and media pressure, which makes crowds increasingly anxious to relate to the modern player.

The Barmy Army, England's singing-and-chanting travelling supporters, have received some flak for destroying the traditional atmosphere of the game, but I for one am grateful for their support.

There is a new set of England cricketers coming through, such as Mark Ilott and Dominic Cork, who are determined to enjoy Test cricket, despite all the pressures. They have grown up, like me, wondering why some star players don't seem to welcome the achievement, the fame and the adulation. Crowds love to sense that enjoyment.

Australian crowds are notorious for their barracking of England players – from Douglas Jardine in the Bodyline series, more than sixty years ago, to Phil Tufnell during England's last two tours. But the most moving reception I've ever received was in the one-day international in Melbourne after I fractured my foot, and I was carried off to applause because everybody knew that my tour was over.

The worst crowd response I have ever known was that at Headingley during the Benson & Hedges Cup quarter-final against Worcestershire last season. We were shot out for less than 100, lost by a mile, and were booed off. Batting had been a liability before lunch on a damp pitch. Some spectators need to engage brain before mouth.

D: Dreams

From the first time I started kicking or throwing a ball, it was my dream to play sport for England. Cricket, football, athletics – you name it, I couldn't get enough of it.

At school, I captained football, cricket, rugby and athletics. I also played badminton, but not as captain. Four jobs was enough to be going along with. I was also into the high jump, and I can still remember a stumpy figure finishing fourth in a Barnsley schools competition!

Now I read about kids as young as seven being surreptitiously approached by top football clubs, and it seems a world apart from the back streets of Barnsley. I didn't specialise in any one sport. I didn't want to – I revelled in everything I tried. My dreams were free to wander wherever they fancied. To have actually been approached by, say, Manchester United or Blackburn Rovers, might have been too much of a shock. I'm not sure whether I could have handled it.

If you have the ability, never abandon your dreams. Only last summer Alan Wells made his Test debut for England at the age of thirty-three. Three years ago, no one would have believed I would play for England, but my Test caps are already in double figures. Try to believe that one day your dreams will happen. Abandon hope, and you abandon opportunity.

Football was my first love, but gradually it became clear that cricket offered the chance of fulfilling my dreams. My eyes flooded with tears when I was told about my Yorkshire debut.

The thrill of my first appearance for England, in a Texaco Trophy international against New Zealand, was indescribable. From that day, I could put the words 'Yorkshire and England' on my sponsored car. I'd rather have no writing on my car at all, but if that is the way it is, then nothing is better than saying that you've represented your country.

Keith Fletcher was England's coach and when he told me I was playing I just went weak. Nerves soon took a hold, and it was a relief to get my first over out of the way.

On all my three debuts – one-day international, Test debut, and overseas debut – I kissed the England badge. It meant that much to me. When Michael Slater kissed his helmet when he scored a Test century against England at Lord's in 1993, the Press wrote that they wished England players would also behave as if a dream had come true. Well, many feel that way. When I got a half-century at Old Trafford in my first Test, I kissed the helmet – missed the badge, but I did kiss the helmet.

Whatever people said, I always believed that one day I would play for England. I've been privileged to be right. No one can ever take that away from me.

E: Effort

Ever since Raymond Illingworth became chairman of selectors, England's players have had the need for effort drummed into them. Illy is adamant that when you come off the field at close of play you should be physically and mentally shattered. He emphasises the point before the start of every Test.

International cricket is no place for coasting, and you should develop the same competitive attitude to every game you play. The time to impress these days is between the ages of twelve and eighteen. Professionals are becoming younger every year, so you should be eager to show how good you are from the start.

If you think that you should be playing in a higher standard, don't take things easy, prove it. Your aim should be to do better every week, not just now and then, and produce the performances to justify your high opinion of yourself.

Above all, England players are sensitive to the suggestion that they are not giving a hundred per cent. On occasions, it is fair to accuse us of a lack of application, perhaps for a loose shot or a lapse of concentration in the field. But anybody not pulling his weight would be out of the England dressing room in a shot.

In the first Test against South Africa in Pretoria last winter, Angus Fraser and Jack Russell were so intent on eking out a few more valuable runs as England's last pair that they wanted to stay on despite an approaching electrical storm. Their effort was undeniable, and it took the good sense of the umpire, Cyril Mitchley, to make them leave the field for their own safety. In the next Test in Jo'burg, the match-saving partnership of Russell and Michael Atherton was nothing short of inspirational.

Some players have such an abundance of talent that a sense of effort rarely shines through. David Gower and Mark Waugh are two Test batsmen of modern times who fit that description. Other batsmen – Geoffrey Boycott in his day, Atherton and Mark Taylor, the Australian captain – are obviously striving with every sinew.

My own game relies on a high intensity. If I throttle back, perhaps because I'm carrying a slight injury, it's rare that I can achieve the same level of success. At times that might make things difficult for me, but a sense of effort does communicate itself to the crowd.

Toiling away for hours in the field does make heavy demands, and there are times when effort begins to slip. That is why it is essential to learn how to switch on and off at the right time. Slip fielders are better at this than most, but out in the deep, seemingly miles away from the crowd or the game, it is easy to start daydreaming. There have been times, I have to admit, when I've had my back to the game when the ball has been bowled. Often, the ball comes your way when you least expect it. I would have looked a real blockhead.

F: Family

Without the enthusiasm and support from my mum and dad, Christine and Trevor, there is every chance that England would never have heard of me. The odds are that I would have been playing Minor Counties cricket for Norfolk, trying to hold down a full-time job as well as enjoying the chance to play cricket at a reasonable standard.

Mum and Dad were willing to make sacrifices as soon as they recognised my interest in sport. They had not much sporting background themselves, but they soon became used to the weekly routine – loading all my equipment into the back of the car, and driving me to all parts of Yorkshire. All their spare time – and money – seemed to be spent in giving their three kids the best start in life they could.

Even so, nobody really imagined that I would one day play cricket for England, and so it was that when I was sixteen they moved to Caister-on-Sea on the Norfolk coast. It was the chance for the family to sample a quieter and more relaxed lifestyle away from the declining heavy industries of South Yorkshire. Everything was settled. My brother and sister had started school and I was the proud possessor of a letter from Barnsley FC recommending me for a trial at Norwich City.

We had barely been at Caister two minutes when my cricket career began to show signs of life. I was chosen for the

My disappointment at leaving the Australia tour early because of my injury was eased by the joy of seeing my son, Liam, for the first time. Anna looks relieved to see me back to help!

Yorkshire Cricket Association under-19 side and was desperate to show what I could do.

The family rallied round superbly. I immediately went back to Barnsley to live with my grandma in Grimethorpe. My parents didn't want to be away from me at such a crucial time in my life and, before too long, the rest of the family followed, all cramming into my other grandma's house in Barnsley until they managed to find a house. They have lived in Monk Bretton, near Barnsley, ever since.

Any young cricketer who has family backing like that has got to be grateful! But there are similar things going on throughout the country every day of the year. When you are growing up, it's all too easy to take it for granted, but try to step back a little from time to time and show recognition of the commitment being put in on your behalf.

Nowadays, of course, 'family' also means my wife, Anna, and

young son, Liam. Their love and understanding are equally important in supporting my cricket career. Anna's father, John, has also been of enormous benefit, especially when it comes to American-style psychology! Not too many American accents are heard around the county grounds of England but when John shouts, 'Hurting time, Darren!' I know it's time to put in a little extra effort.

Babies can be a real headache for anybody playing professional sport. It is important to ensure that you do not suffer from disturbed nights and arrive bleary-eyed and weary for a vital game. Anna always took it upon herself to get up in the middle of the night. Anyway, if I've bowled twenty overs that day, it will take an earthquake to disturb me.

G: Gamesmanship

Why don't players walk any more? I've persistently been asked that question since the day I made my first-class debut. The simplest answer is that our sporting ethics reflect the society in which we live, and that life is much more competitive than it was many years ago. The desire to win often tempts people to ride their good fortune whenever they can.

It is easy to insist that batsmen should walk when they are playing for England, but much harder to achieve. The hopes of millions of people are at stake. Within the team, the result of months of hard work might depend upon a single moment. Generally, if I have nicked a ball, I like to walk, but I would never claim I'm able to do it every time.

I reckon spinners are most hard done by. Some dubious umpiring decisions for bat-pad catches fall their way from time to time but, on balance, I reckon they get far less than they deserve. Slight nicks on to pads, or minor deflections off gloves, are so hard to spot.

Because of that, I tend to walk for bat-pad catches. You would think that, being a fast bowler, I would rather support my own fast bowlers' union, but not a bit of it! Last summer, for example, I was convinced that I had Keith Arthurton caught behind during the Lord's Test, but it was given 'not out'. In such circumstances, the temptation for the batsman is to await the umpire's decision, in the hope that you even up your luck. Win a few, lose a few. On the county circuit, there is a majority view that, if you take that attitude, it all evens out in the end.

The Australians, almost without exception, await the umpire's decision. The umpires are in sole charge, so they believe in letting them get on with it. English attitudes are gradually moving into line. Why should we be expected to do the umpires' job for them?

Modern Test players don't really expect batsmen to walk. There is always some grumbling, but I agree with Alec Stewart, England's vice-captain. He always insists that sledging a batsman for not walking is out of order, because the batsman has every right to leave the decision to the umpire. As such, it could be argued that even if he knows that he hit it, he is not being particularly dishonest.

Some players are particularly skilled at making a big show of walking for the obvious edges. In that way, they might convince the umpire that they are an honest sort, and that might just help them get the benefit of the doubt in a borderline case.

So what would I advise a teenager about to make his club debut? Should he be expected to walk? It's a desperately difficult subject, and all I can say is that it is up to the individual's own conscience. He will lose a few friends if he stays at the wicket when he has nicked it, but if he makes a big score, it might get him recognised. He might also suffer a dreadful decision a week later. Sometimes, club players, who only get a bat at best once a week, are even more reluctant to walk for a faint edge.

Appealing can be another touchy area. Australian sides often complain that the Asian Test nations appeal too much. In reply, India, Pakistan and Sri Lanka accuse the Australians of being too aggressive on the field. In a way, both have a point.

The rule adopted by both Yorkshire and England is that, if you are going to appeal, it should be a concerted team effort. The more confident it sounds, the better. I remember some of the half-hearted appeals in club matches – someone should have shouted, 'All together lads, or not at all.' Confident appealing can, very occasionally, tilt an umpire's judgement. And there is nothing in the laws to say that you cannot appeal as loudly as you like.

There are certain players, however, who encourage trust. When Australia are in the field, the Australian Press often judge the likelihood that a player has nicked the ball by the reaction of the captain, Mark Taylor, at first slip. They are convinced that Taylor never appeals if he thinks the batsman is not out. Sometimes, while Ian Healy and the other slips give an appeal all it is worth, Taylor's uncertainty shows through.

Since the introduction of match referees in international

cricket, players' behaviour has markedly improved, and no more so than in the decline of sledging. I believe in aggressive cricket, and would never try to stop bowlers and batsmen exchanging the odd word. But insults from the slips or short leg are a different matter.

If Durham's captain, Michael Roseberry, is a contender as the noisiest short leg in the world, the Australian, David Boon, must be the quietest. I like to talk when I'm batting, but during the last Ashes tour he just stared at me as if every word was the most foolish I had ever spoken. Sometimes I wondered if he was sledging me in silence!

Craig McDermott, the Australian fast bowler, was much more abusive, especially when I hit him for four. I used to laugh at him, and poke my tongue out, which didn't always go down too well. But nobody held any grudges, and I was taken aback to read in *The Cricketer* magazine a few months later that he listed me as one of the players he most admired. It is rare that on-the-field aggression spills over into the evening.

Lively banter between team-mates is acceptable, and there is no more skilful duo in the English game than Steve Rhodes and Richard Illingworth, wicketkeeper and left-arm spinner respectively for both Worcestershire and England. They are cocky, not abusive, constantly telling each other that they have a batsman's measure, and that a wicket is on its way. It all increases the pressure, and is within the rules. They make an excellent team.

Umpires in club, or school, cricket, might not allow the same leeway. There are always limits of acceptability, and you need to know where the umpire draws them. Australian fast bowlers spending a summer in England have often shocked English club players by how much they dish out crude verbal attacks.

Another gambit that pays off is when the South African side speak in Afrikaans. You feel that they are abusing you, even if they are just commenting about the weather. I often think it would be worthwhile learning a few key words – bouncer, yorker and so on – so you would be in position to play the shot long before the ball had left the bowler's hand.

Claiming catches when you know that they have bounced is totally out of order. This is one area where players' honesty at first-class level is generally of a high standard, and I would urge youngsters beginning the game to adopt the same approach. However, don't always instantly condemn a player who claims a catch that TV replays show fell just short. Occasionally, when diving for a catch which arrives on the half-volley the fielder does not always know whether the ball carried.

One more piece of gamesmanship worth mentioning is when a bowler runs out a batsman at the bowler's end for backing up too much. As a general rule, forget it. There is nothing more pathetic than a bowler stopping at the stumps and threatening to take off the bails. Just get on with bowling the ball.

If you are playing, say, in a 20-over Evening Cup game, and someone is persistently nicking yardage, then issue a quiet warning, and make sure the umpire hears it. If he continues to do it, then you may have to run him out. But it is not a particularly welcome sight, and the least you can do is not make a song and dance about it.

H: Humour

Old Test stars always complain that young players of today don't seem to enjoy themselves as much any more. Well, I've got news for them. There is a new breed of player emerging in the England side, determined to cope with the pressure and experience the fun that should be part and parcel of playing cricket for your country.

On the A tour to South Africa in 1993, we had a squad that revelled in light-hearted moments, and also became highly successful on the field. I had always enjoyed the company of players such as Dominic Cork and Mark Ilott from England under-19 games, and other people on that tour, such as the Glamorgan all-rounder, Robert Croft, proved to be a bit of a joker. Michael Vaughan, my Yorkshire team-mate, tells me that the mood in India the following winter was just as good and contributed to the most successful A tour ever.

England A tours have played an important part in encouraging players to enjoy cricket at a higher level. They are a halfway house to the full England side, important, but less intense than playing for the full Test side. Develop a positive attitude here – learn, for example, how to respond sensibly to the media – and the experience can be invaluable.

In Australia, I enjoyed playing to the crowd, or playing to the TV cameras, and I got a warm-hearted response in return. The opposite response is to mope around, complaining persistently about the pressure you are under, and letting such negative thoughts affect your game. Behave like that, and one day you will wake up and find that your England career is over, and that you never got around to enjoying it.

The English media loves my relaxed attitude when I'm doing well, and then snipes at me for not taking the game seriously if things go badly. That annoys me. If my attitude is applauded in the good times, then it should not be slated just because my wickets have dried up. I think I've encouraged a fresher, more open attitude in English cricket, and I'm not going to change.

The advantages of such camaraderie for a side are obvious. If you are going through a rough time on the field, and someone makes you laugh, everyone gets a buzz for another ten minutes. When Yorkshire were on a low at the start of the 1990s, if things were going badly the atmosphere would be dead. We were a side short of characters, scrabbling around for confidence, exuberance and spirit. Every day became a drag. By 1995, players like Paul Grayson (unfortunately now with Essex), Mark Robinson and Michael Vaughan had helped to establish a new spirit. Watch closely the next time you see Yorkshire and, in a quieter moment, you might even spot one of our games of imaginary football!

Against Lancashire, during my first season in the Yorkshire side, I played a beautiful forward-defensive shot against Mike Watkinson. 'Winker' raised an eyebrow and said in his rich Lancashire accent, 'Has your dad brought your camera?' One-liners like that crease me up.

Peter Hartley is one Yorkshire player with a wry sense of humour. Any captain asking him what field he wants is likely to get the answers, 'A bigger field' or 'Chesterfield', where the ball seams and he always takes wickets. Mark Robinson's jokes are so old that they must have all come from silent comedies.

Last summer, in England, I occasionally couldn't resist a trick that I had learned from Shane Warne. Just before he bowled the last ball of the day in the Melbourne Test, he put his tongue out and pulled his face at me. Admittedly, it was a bit cheeky, but I couldn't resist trying it out on Mark Nicholas when Yorkshire played Hampshire. It's fair to say the slip fielders saw the joke more than Mark!

I'd urge every young player starting out not to forget that sport is meant to be enjoyed. Viewed properly, it can leave you with a lifetime's memories, and many friends. As well as making a joke, always be prepared to take one. Paul Grayson's jokes can be close to the mark, but he is always happy to take stick in return. I also

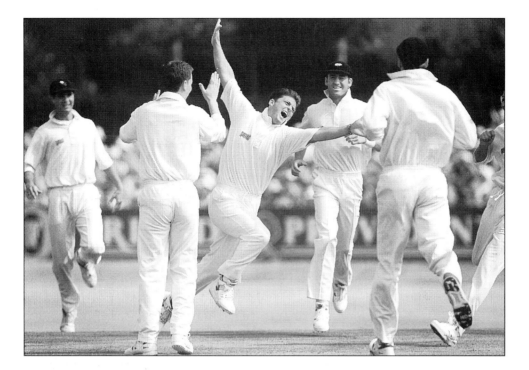

An outrageous banking aeroplane celebration to mark my dismissal of Michael Atherton during Yorkshire's 1995 NatWest quarter-final win.

get a lot of stick – you just have to look at the previous chapter to recognise that. It all helps the world go round.

I: Injuries

Injuries are the curse of every sportsman and woman. When fitness does become a problem, the advice of a good physio is of enormous benefit. The judgement and honesty of Wayne Morton, who is the physiotherapist for both Yorkshire and England, has been invaluable to me.

It is important that there is a trusting relationship between a professional cricketer and his physio. The player must be honest about the problems he is encountering, and the physio must be truthful about the likely diagnosis. That can create a bond which can last throughout a career.

There have been times when Wayne has advised me as if I was his own son, and I appreciate him for that. He has fostered my career as much as anyone.

Wayne is a hard taskmaster, but his positive treatment of all my injuries has prevented me from lapsing into depression. Early in my career, I suffered two stress fractures of my back,

165

and Wayne warned me that one day I might need an operation. Fortunately, touch wood, that has not been necessary.

When I dislocated my ankle, I returned from the hospital on crutches. Wayne was aghast, and his treatment was such that I was playing again within six days, with absolutely no ill effects. He wanted me back on the field as soon as possible. I felt some pain for a while, but he knew there were no long-term dangers.

However, when there has been a risk to my long-term fitness, he has also protected me. When I suffered a side strain, there was pressure for me to return after three weeks; Wayne would not take the risk and ensured that I did not play for six. He was concerned, on my behalf, about the possible long-term damage.

Last summer, I became caught up in a difference of opinion between Yorkshire and England over a foot injury, a leftover from the fracture that I had suffered on the previous winter's Ashes tour, and which forced me to miss the Old Trafford Test. England, understandably, wanted me to rest until I was fit enough to return to Test cricket. But all the scans and independent medical reports that Wayne had requested indicated that an odd one-day match for Yorkshire would not impair my recovery. That allowed me to play in Yorkshire's NatWest quarter-final win against Lancashire at Headingley, one of the greatest experiences of my county career. I felt that I owed Yorkshire that one, and my return to fitness was not affected as a result.

After fracturing my foot in Australia, I still had doubts about my fitness all last summer. There was always a nagging fear in the back of my mind that I might break down again, and a repeat of that injury might have ended my career. Even when you have returned to the side, the mental scars can take much longer to heal. Not that the media, or the public, are prepared to make allowances for that.

Physios also have to be amateur psychologists. Wayne senses the difference between a real and imagined injury, differentiating between those players who ache so much that they need a rub-down, and those who just like the idea of a massage. On England's A tour to South Africa, there was a time when I never thought I would play a first-class game, but Wayne ensured that I remained optimistic. In the end, I played in the A Test, and made a bit of an impression.

Wayne is a big factor in the Yorkshire dressing room. He makes people believe in their ability. I'm sure that he can do the same for England.

Young players persistently ignore injuries, just assuming that they will go away. Don't. Be aware of your body and the warnings it is giving you. Proper treatment is easily available, and that means more than just wrapping a bandage around the bit that is hurting.

When I was a teenager, I played cricket nearly every day of the week. When I wasn't playing matches, I was netting, often on hard indoor surfaces. The result was that at eighteen, I had my first of two stress fractures. Some wear and tear is inevitable for professionals, but young players deserve looking after. Schools and clubs who run young players into the ground are doing the game a great disservice.

J: Journeys

Cricket has given me opportunities to travel that I could never have imagined. England's tour of South Africa last winter was already my fifth visit to the country, at the age of twenty-five. I've been to Australia twice, New Zealand, Holland (albeit only for a weekend), as well as spending every summer rushing the length and breadth of England. Not so long ago, even travelling around England was a real eye-opener for me. I had never eaten Chinese, Indian or Italian food until I started playing cricket for Yorkshire. I'd hardly heard an accent outside South Yorkshire. Sussex might have been a foreign land.

Limited-overs internationals are becoming ever more popular, but thankfully the hectic shuttling between venues at the end of the South Africa tour, which took in seven towns and cities in thirteen days as we prepared for the World Cup, is a rarity.

Anybody who imagines all that flying must be fun is severely mistaken. It is immensely wearing. On long journeys, you can even pick up injuries just sitting on a plane. When I returned from Australia with a fractured foot, on the journey home I developed a small blood clot in my left calf because I had to leave my foot in the air. England's players are advised to stand up and move around for at least half an hour in every three-hour period. We even have suggested exercises that we can do in our seats.

Other sports don't have it so good. English footballers playing in European competition barely have time to find out the price of a beer. For one European tie in Scandinavia last autumn, Nottingham Forest returned so quickly after the final whistle that, with the help of a small time difference, they were back at East Midlands airport by around midnight! Not much time for sightseeing there.

Even the least adventurous cricket tourist manages to sample the inside of a few bars and restaurants. On the coast, rare days off might be spent on the nearest beach. With the help of England's sponsor, Tetley Bitter, trips are arranged to game parks or wineries.

Golf is also a passion for many players, and my chance to play eighteen holes around Royal Melbourne, one of the world's best courses, ranks as one of the greatest social events of my life.

In South Africa, I have been speechless at the vast gulf between rich and poor. People who think they live in poverty in England might change their mind if they saw some of the South African townships. Maybe I was naive, but I didn't realise that families of seven or eight lived in a tin hut no bigger than the size of a garden shed. The chance to play cricket in Soweto last winter, hopefully bring a little pleasure, and be introduced to the president, Nelson Mandela, was something I shall always cherish.

Travelling enables you to make friends worldwide, and gives you the chance to abandon some of your fears and prejudices. Equally, you become aware of different characteristics of each country. I found many New Zealanders very quiet and polite, sometimes even lacklustre. But Australians – or at least a surprising number of them – have been brought up to be loud, brash and aggressive.

K: Kidology

One area of the game that young players often overlook is kidology. It is another simple way of trying to outwit your opponents – persuading them that you are a superior player with nothing more than a few words, or even just a glance in their direction. The more character and personality you dare to show in your cricket, the more you can make kidology a useful weapon.

Every time the ball passes the outside edge, a basic form of kidology takes place. The batsman generally tries to act as if he is totally unconcerned, making out that he was not really playing a shot, and that everything was under control. The bowler, meanwhile, will be throwing his hands to the heavens as if he has witnessed the biggest slice of luck in the history of the game. Both are seeking to establish an advantage for the next ball.

On a flat pitch, a bowler's kidology skills are particularly important. Shane Warne, Australia's world-class leg-spinner, is a master of little ooohs and aahs, and peers at a batsman's technique – all intended to communicate the feeling that he is spinning a web from which the batsman has no escape.

One amusing moment during Australia's first Test against Pakistan in Brisbane last November sums up what I'm saying. Before he bowled the last ball of the day to Basit Ali, Warne became involved in a long conversation with Steve Waugh and his captain, Mark Taylor, as if discussing Basit's fatal flaw. They were probably just talking about what bar they might go to later. Basit, trying to show that he would not fall for such kidology, gave one of the biggest winks ever seen on a cricket ground, and managed to survive.

The best team in the world at kidology are the West Indians, with the Australians not far behind. The West Indies' four fast bowlers will consistently behave as if they are the most frightening fast bowlers in the world. Even in their most unguarded moments, they never forget the advantages to be had by intimidating opposing batsmen. All their pre-tour publicity is intended to unsettle key players in the other team.

Every time an England side arrives in Australia, all the old names who have starred against England in the past – Dennis Lillee, Jeff Thomson, Greg and Ian Chappell, and now Allan Border – are wheeled out on celebrity golf days to express their belief that the Poms are no good, and are heading for a stuffing. There is so much hype that they might be promoting a heavyweight boxing match.

Even the Australian media love to play their part in bringing down a Pommie touring team. They delight in making an England player feel vulnerable before he has even got on to the pitch. They loved the eyeball-to-eyeball confrontation stage-managed between me and Merv Hughes before the start of the Ashes series. 'Hello, Mr Hughes,' I said to him. 'I've heard a lot about you.' He was so shocked, he could hardly get a word out.

Australian players are not afraid of using kidology before a match. To our mind, they sound dangerously over-confident, shouting the odds before a ball has been bowled. We are wary of making too many predictions, in case everything blows back in our faces. While we just settle for saying we are 'hopeful' that we'll do well, the Aussies are saying that they are the better side.

It does not have to sound boastful. But it does demand a fair

'Hello, Mr Hughes, I've heard a lot about you.' My face-to-face with Big Merv in Canberra at the official launch of the Ashes tour.

share of cheek and confidence. Perhaps that's why I'm all in favour of it.

L: Loneliness

Combating loneliness – or homesickness – is one of the least recognised problems facing a Test cricketer. The merest complaint about the 'hardships' of playing for England brings an avalanche of criticism from the public, and understandably so. But however glamorous the life can seem, there are times when the home life you have left behind really is worth dreaming about. Four-month tours are a different proposition to a two-week package holiday.

My trip to Australia two winters ago was particularly taxing. It was my first full England tour, and I lapped up every minute of it, but when I left West Yorkshire, Anna, my wife, was eight months pregnant. Hardly perfect planning! Liam was eventually born on the eve of the first Test in Brisbane. Anna was bursting to tell me the news, but waited until it was a decent hour in the morning before giving me a call.

It is when the loneliness really bites that you need support. For a time, in the early 1990s, England even had a chaplain close to hand, the Rev. Andrew Wingfield-Digby, a Minor Counties cricketer, active figure in the Christians in Sport movement, and universally known in the cricketing world as 'Wingers-Diggers'.

There are normally a couple of team-mates who can also lift your spirits, although no one wants to risk dragging down the positive mood of the party. Everybody is missing something: weddings, birthdays, anniversaries or other important family occasions. It is down to each individual player to combat attacks of homesickness in their own way – and they must be contained if form is not to suffer and the tour is going to be successful. Some players have family pictures by the bed, others prefer to bury them in the suitcase. Everybody must cope in his own way.

England's record overseas has not been good in recent years, but I wouldn't go as far as to blame it on homesickness. Otherwise Raymond Illingworth will be picking a squad of single blokes, and I'm not ready to step down just yet!

When I'm down, I don't like to phone home. Your close family are experiencing just as unsettling a time, and it is unfair to expect somebody to be able to give you a boost from thousands of miles away. Often you just pass your depression down the phone line! I always ring England when I'm feeling happy and optimistic.

England normally allow wives, children and girlfriends to come out for a few weeks during the tour. In South Africa last winter, everybody visited at Christmas, which gave us all something to look forward to. But for the good of team spirit limitations of two to three weeks have to be imposed. After-

Nowhere is more lonely than a deserted airport departure lounge, with only a pair of crutches for company.

match discussions are rarely as successful when players are under orders from their wives to make that 8 p.m. dinner booking.

Australia have recently broken with tradition by allowing all their players single rooms. Money is no longer quite as tight in the game. But I've never objected to sharing a room. At least it gives you someone to yatter away to.

M: Media

Nobody likes criticism, but some people handle it better than others. That's the age-old truth about dealing with the media. The relationship between a professional sportsman and the media will, in general, always be prone to difficulties, but there is no point becoming obsessive about it. Everybody has a job to do, and if we all just got on with doing it well there would be fewer problems.

Within a general feeling of wariness, there will always be many individual players and members of the media who maintain a friendship or rapport. As long as I have developed a basic respect for a journalist or broadcaster's judgement and fairness, then I'm not going to lose sleep over what they say about me.

At least that's the basic idea. Constructive criticism I can handle. But wild attacks just for the sake of a good headline annoy me. And when it comes to nosing into a player's private life, then I get as resentful as the next person. I can't really believe that anyone wants to see a picture of me in a nightclub or a cinema. Surely they want to see me taking wickets for England?

During the West Indies series in 1995, I attended an official promotional evening on the Tuesday evening before the Old Trafford Test on behalf of Bell's whisky. We did not even know that a Manchester photographer was there – not until we picked up a tabloid on the Thursday morning (the first day of the Test) and saw a story that implied we'd been sloshing back whisky the previous evening. That's the sort of misrepresentation that damages relationships. It's so easy for players to retaliate with a prolonged vow of silence.

I've had a good press, especially in Australia in 1994–5. I'd be lying if I said I didn't enjoy the headlines. But the exuberance I was praised for when I was taking wickets for England was held the following summer to be irresponsibility when I was not. In reality, all that had happened was that I had suffered a serious injury and lost form.

Generally, I've found the local Yorkshire media more critical than the national media, and relationships between the two sides have never been as hospitable as they should be. After consistently harsh judgements in the papers, few Yorkshire players have much desire to talk cricket to reporters after close of play and hear the same old arguments going round in circles.

Players beginning their first-class career deserve a bit more patience and support than those who have already made it into the Test side. But, all too often, Yorkshire players are judged by the glory days of the past when championships were all but inevitable. These days that is an unrealistic stance to take – the championship is far more competitive. Still, there is one advantage. After the stick you can cop at county level, getting used to the pressures with England is no problem!

N: No-balls

Every youngster who has ever watched a Test match on the TV with his dad will have had cause to wonder at one time or another what all the tut-tutting and stomping off to put the kettle on was all about. The answer will probably have been that an England bowler has been no-balling again. It might even have been me.

If anything is designed to annoy an experienced cricket watcher it is a first-class cricketer bowling no-balls. It is regarded as an insult to the game. Everybody knows there is no excuse for it, but it happens. It is annoying enough in Test cricket, but in limited-overs matches (when the extra ball becomes even more crucial) it can easily decide the outcome.

Nobody bowls a no-ball on purpose. 'Ho-ho, then why are there so many of them?' I hear you say. Well, here is the case for the defence and, before I begin, I've got to add that most of these excuses don't count for spinners!

The variety of cricket grounds we play on is enormous. No approach to the wicket is exactly the same. Undulating grounds abound, all possessing their own extra challenge. Many squares have had around a hundred years of top dressing applied every autumn and so lie slightly above the level of the rest of the ground. At Old Trafford, for example, the square is on a slight ridge and therefore difficult to handle. Many other factors disturb a bowler's rhythm. There may be a blustery wind, which constantly changes both force and direction and makes hitting the line consistently ever more difficult.

A bowler may also be asked to switch ends, and so might suddenly get the chance to bowl downhill when he has been bowling uphill in his earlier spell. Every knowledgeable bowler realises that a downhill run can often cause no-balls, but moving the marker back a fraction does not always seem to work.

When a bowler intends to slip in a quicker delivery, the extra effort entailed often means that he oversteps. If he is especially pumped up during a spell, perhaps because the match is in the balance, or because he has taken a particular dislike to the batsman, he can also waste his efforts with another no-ball.

Sometimes, no-balling can even be put down simply to a lack of form, perhaps because a bowler has just recovered from injury, or he is about to succumb to one, or just because he is stale with too much cricket.

People also scoff at bowlers constantly over-stepping in the nets. Some bowlers deliver the ball about two yards over the line, which can't do anybody any good. Raymond Illingworth is not the first chairman of selectors to try to clamp down on this, with limited success. All I can say is that it can be very confusing if there is no umpire standing there.

But there is an overriding rule about excuses about no-balls – and that is that they should never, under any circumstances, be used. Like it or not, it is a bowler's job not to bowl them.

Develop a consistently smooth run, and mark it out carefully. If it helps, use two bowling markers like I do – one at the beginning of the run and one when you break into your full stride. If you no-ball, ask yourself why and try to remedy the fault immediately.

Try to wipe it from your game. And good luck.

O: Opportunity

'Fancy a bowl, son?' I wonder how many of you can remember the first occasion you were asked that. For many youngsters, it is a signal for the heart to pound, nerves to flutter, and hands sweat so badly that letting the ball go in vaguely the right direction becomes an achievement in itself.

Nerves have prevented many good players from achieving their true potential. Opportunities, instead of being eagerly sought, are shied away from. At the time, it might seem all too easy to opt for a quiet life.

But the fact is that opportunities must always be grasped. Every time you feel yourself affected by nerves, remind yourself that this is your opportunity to prove you can handle the pressure, and that you are not about to let yourself down lightly. Debuts, at whatever level, can be the most daunting of all, but there is nothing better than creating a good impression from the off.

If you blow your chance because, in hindsight, you were not quite good enough, then there is no shame in that. But never miss out because you bottled it, or when the time came you were not properly prepared. As a host of England players (nearly all batsmen) with just one Test cap can testify, opportunity may only knock once.

You might regard yourself as, say, a middle-order batsman. But if a captain offers you the chance to open the innings, or maybe bowl some leg-spinners, jump at the chance to see what you can do. No career is set in stone, especially for a young player. Arnie Sidebottom first attracted Yorkshire's interest as an opening batsman, but he developed into such an adept seam bowler in the 'eighties that he ended up playing for England. Occasionally, too, Yorkshire asked Arnie to fulfil an emergency role as an opening batsman again and he always did so with great courage and not a little skill. Recognising opportunities within a match situation is also vital. If a bowler is flagging, make sure you take full advantage with some quick runs. If you have the chance of a run-out, don't blow it with a lazy misfield. If there is a chance, as a captain, to bring on a certain bowler for tactical reasons, don't dwell on it until it is too late.

Throughout England, thousands of volunteers run coaching sessions, supervise junior sides, or take umpiring courses. It is their commitment that gives a chance to so many. Never treat that chance lightly.

Opportunities have never been greater in Yorkshire cricket. The commitment to the Park Avenue cricket academy gives talented young players their best chance ever to make the grade. Players lucky enough to gain an academy place should never take their own talents lightly.

Much is often made of the distinction between England and

If you get
the opportunity
for some
specialised
coaching, take
it. These Priory
School cricketers
are taking part
in a fielding
session.

Australian selection methods. England tend to give more players the chance of Test cricket, which leads to a certain amount of chopping and changing. In unsuccessful summers, it has been known for as many as thirty players to represent England.

The Australians, though, probably because their first-class system is not as extensive, being limited to only half a dozen sides, show greater faith in an individual player once they have selected him. Opportunity, in their eyes, is more likely to mean at least a full series than a single Test.

P: Professionalism

Professionalism has become a tainted word – linked, for example, in football's 'professional foul', to a deliberate attempt to stop an opponent by unfair means. But most professional attitudes are to be encouraged and there is no reason why many of them cannot be adopted for life from a young age.

Professionalism is about so many things. It demands total honesty about your performance, and not making pathetic excuses for being late to a game, or for dropping a catch, or for missing a straight ball. It is also about conducting yourself in the proper manner, always playing the game hard but fair. It is as much about how you think as how you act.

Far less important is whether your blazer is neatly pressed, or whether you have one or two days' stubble on your chin, whatever the sticklers for traditional dress standards might think. I'm sure that Yorkshire's overseas professional, Michael Bevan, will agree with me on that one!

Embittered old county professionals – now no longer as common, perhaps, as twenty years ago – who complain and criticise from their corner of a dressing room, are doing a disservice to their trade. Their knowledge should be enthusiastically shared with young players at every opportunity, not hidden away out of envy at a career that has just begun. The same is true of every club or village side in the land: older players in the side should recognise a responsibility to encourage, not knock, the next generation.

Paul Grayson's departure for Essex, I reckon, is a great loss to Yorkshire. His decision was both regrettable and understandable. Too often, at the end of a net session, players would begin to troop away absentmindedly before he had had a chance to have a bat. He was a junior player, but deserved a more professional outlook.

High standards of professionalism are seen in the likes of Alan Wells, whose years of dignified and diligent service for Sussex were finally rewarded, as he approached his mid-thirties, with a Test cap against the West Indies last summer. His first-ball dismissal will haunt him for ever, but no one can take away the fact that he played for England.

One overseas player who has been a true professional is the West Indies fast bowler, Courtney Walsh, whose efforts on behalf of Gloucestershire have been unstinting, and who has always been willing to pass on advice. Every player is focused in the middle of a Test match; show me a player, such as Courtney, who remembers his obligations on a bleak early May afternoon in Derby, and I'll show you a true professional.

Professionalism is not about everybody following the same rigid routine. Individual players require individual training routines, to suit both their character and their role in the side, and it is this recognition that is at the heart of England's current thinking.

You could not see two more different characters than Alec Stewart (who is meticulously orderly) and Michael Atherton (who occasionally brings to mind the observation about the former England batsman, Colin Milburn, looking like an unmade bed), but England's captain and vice-captain are both excellent professionals in their own way.

Many topics covered in this book – such as diet, fitness and practice – are all concerned with adopting a proper approach.

Professionalism should not lead to a team of clones, bereft of flair and imagination. But it demands that each player recognises his responsibilities to the game and to his team-mates. That is equally true at every level.

Q: Questions

For as long as cricket has been played, all too often there has been a gulf between knowledgeable older players and youngsters just starting out and eager to learn. Whether the relationship occurs at Test level, or the smallest village side, the outcome is sadly often the same. The young player is too timid to seek advice, and the senior player is often reluctant to offer it unless invited. The result is that knowledge does not pass between the generations as automatically as it should.

I'm at a stage in my career where I can understand the emotions on both sides. I'm regarded as a pretty up-front, straightforward bloke, but there have still been many times in my career when I've wanted to talk to a great player about the art of fast bowling, but not dared to ask. I just hoped that they might suddenly take it upon themselves to wander over and begin talking about the game.

Now that I have played for England, the situation is often reversed, and I frequently find myself wanting to advise younger, up-and-coming players on an aspect of their game. But the suspicion is that they might not want to listen, so often the opportunity passes.

Chris Silverwood, Yorkshire's young seam bowler, asked me about how I bowl my slower ball. Often, I bowl an off-spinner – sometimes even a leg-spinner. I was delighted to explain my methods. Not everybody does things the same way, but the discussion might have helped Chris to sort out in his own mind the way he wants to go about things.

That was a straightforward case of team-mates helping each other out, but cricket also has a proud tradition of players from different sides – often different countries – revelling in the chance to discuss their particular speciality. Shane Warne's discussions with the former Pakistani leg-spinner, Abdul Qadir, during the 1994 Australian tour, is an example of the benefits that can occur when two great players fall into conversation. In the middle of a fiercely contested Ashes series, I still took time to chat to Warne about how he handled the media, and to Craig McDermott about how he keeps his strong wrist action – the key to his success as a fast bowler.

Young players must dare to ask questions. They will rarely be rejected, and if they are, it will be the senior player whose reputation suffers. Phil Carrick, Yorkshire's ex-left-arm spinner, used to work with Jeremy Batty (an off-spinner now with Somerset) as if they were brother and sister! He had to do a bit of laundry for 'Fergie', mind you, by way of return.

Don't just ask technical questions. For a young player, learning the mental side of the game can be equally important. Once you've asked the question, weigh up how valuable the answer is to your particular career. Michael Holding wrote last summer that I should lengthen my run. I weighed it up, decided it was worth a try, but eventually returned to my old style.

From time to time I'm inundated with letters from prospective fast bowlers, asking me for advice. I'm embarrassed to admit that often I just don't have the time to reply. The few spare hours I get during the year I'm desperate to organise my own life, and spend some time with my wife and family. Hopefully, many of those questions will have been answered in this book.

People might ask how to bowl an inswinger, or outswinger, or how to achieve reverse swing. Without seeing a player bowl, it is difficult to offer sensible personal advice. The basic methods for such deliveries should be easy to discover from a host of coaches and coaching books.

I've taken advice from many people: Peter Lever, Fred Trueman, Michael Holding, Craig McDermott, Ian Botham, Dennis Lillee, Neil Foster, Geoffrey Boycott, Bob Willis and all the Yorkshire coaches. They might say, 'Well, let's have a look at you.' It's often the only place to start.

R: Respect

Respect the game. You might have heard that occasionally and wondered what on earth the speaker was getting at. As a young player just starting out, success and enjoyment are easy to relate to. Respect, though, tends to come more naturally as you grow older.

Respecting the game means, for example, understanding a

little bit about its history. There is no need to wade through volumes of old *Wisden Cricketers' Almanacks* if that's not quite your scene. But try to be aware of some of the great names of world cricket – W. G. Grace, Ranji, Bradman, Larwood, Ramadhin, Laker, May, Hanif Mohammad, Sobers, Boycott, Lillee, Holding and Botham – and their impact on the game.

It is equally important to develop a respect for cricket's values and traditions. We all know that phrases such as, 'It's just not cricket, old boy,' are now only seriously spoken by tipsy MCC members in panama hats. We all know that, outside the gentlest village matches, cricket is a tough, hard-fought game. But despite endless controversies, its reputation for fair play still survives in reasonable shape. Every time I'm on the verge of losing my rag on the field, the recognition that I'm in danger of setting a bad example helps to hold me back. Well, sometimes.

As a young player, try to respect the knowledge of older players in the side. You might be a better natural player than many of them, but that does not necessarily mean that they have little knowledge of the game. It is at least worth listening to find out. Richie Richardson's performances as Yorkshire's overseas player were below expectations, but we knew what he had achieved for the West Indies, and that his attitude was faultless, so we never lost our respect for him as a person or a player.

Respecting your opponents involves not carrying on-the-field friction into the bar after the game. Cricket should be competi-

Shane Warne and myself might have been rivals in Australia, but I've an enormous respect for a world-class bowler and a smashing bloke.

tive, but don't assume that your opponents are all congenital idiots just because they have been giving you a hard time. Some players feel uncomfortable socialising with opponents during a Test series – they find it hard to psyche themselves up to compete against somebody they have been having a drink with the night before. It's entirely their choice, but it would be a poorer game if everybody took the same view.

Respecting the game, in local cricket, also means doing your fair share of ground duties during a season, such as marking the pitch or pushing the roller, or helping to clear up once a match is finished. Much cricket in England exists through voluntary labour. Deep down people feel that they are doing something useful. Their respect for the game runs deep.

S: Schedule

Demands on Test players have never been higher. Despite a growing recognition that international schedules must be pared back, to protect the health, enthusiasm and fitness of the world's leading players, too much international cricket is still being played.

The example of the world's greatest batsman, Brian Lara, illustrates that only too painfully. Lara went AWOL for a time during the West Indies' tour of England last summer, stating that he had had enough. He soon returned, but was subsequently fined by the West Indies cricket board. That caused such a rift that Lara pulled out of their tour to Australia. What should have been a glorious career was in danger of turning sour.

Lara's indecision over whether to fulfil his contract with Warwickshire was another example of the mental and physical strain he was under. The West Indies tread the international circuit virtually twelve months a year and eventually mental and physical fitness must begin to suffer.

The Australians are equally wary of our extensive county programme, which amounts to about a hundred days of cricket a season: seventeen four-day championship matches, a further seventeen Sunday League games, at least four (and perhaps twice as many) days in the Benson & Hedges Cup, the NatWest Trophy competition, as well as a smattering of festival and benefit commitments.

Australian bowlers have long been dissuaded from playing in

England. The fear is that they will be overbowled and return to Australia either stale or with injury problems. Yet we have to survive such an arduous schedule every single summer. Shane Warne turned down a lucrative deal to play for Northamptonshire in 1995 and Steve Waugh's shunning of Durham's offer for 1996 suggests that many of their Test batsmen equally believe that a rest is more beneficial than a change.

Australia's Ashes tours of England have traditionally lasted throughout the summer, but there are suggestions that they will be pared back in future. Leading Australian players prefer the idea of a brief warm-up to a five-Test series, with only one four-day match in between each Test, and one-day internationals played either at the beginning or the end of the summer. That would probably reduce tours by a month, and protect players from burn-out. England may not be too enthusiastic about the idea, but I reckon that for the sake of players' mental and physical well-being, it is how tours must be drawn up in the future.

The lengthier, old-fashioned tours have become outdated in an age of mass long-haul travel. On our last Ashes tour, the build-up dragged on for ever. Even then, our final match before the first Test in sub-tropical Brisbane was played in wet-and-windy Hobart, which necessitated a temperature change overnight of about 15°C! I'd like to see a players' representative given the chance to air views on itineraries to the TCCB before they are agreed.

One thing I would increase is to stage the World Cup every two years, instead of four. Teams should compete in a league table, with the top four playing off. What could be simpler?

People assumed that between the end of the 1995 English season and our departure for South Africa a month later, I had ample chance to put my feet up. Hardly! During that time, I moved house, had several medical checks on my old foot injury, and kept a constant eye on my fitness. There were sponsorship deals to arrange in liaison with my agents, Advantage International, a book to discuss, measurements in London for official England clothing, and a host of requests on my answerphone every day.

For most of the next five months I would be away from my wife and young son, which demanded all manner of plans and arrangements. In the middle of it all, we managed to grab a couple of days away somewhere. I was almost relieved when the tour began as it gave me time to collect my thoughts.

T: Targets

At the start of my first Australian tour I set myself a target – to join the list of England bowlers who had taken twenty wickets in an Ashes series. Before my fractured foot put an end to it, I was well placed to achieve my aim.

Setting targets can be a useful motivational ploy in all forms of cricket. Cricket is a statistical game, and all you have to do is decide upon your minimum aim, either over a match or a season, to use this to your advantage.

In an individual innings, many batsmen maintain their concentration by counting their runs in groups of ten. Every landmark up to, say, fifty, represents another little achievement. After that, they might not count as much.

But targets can also be set over the course of a season. The first aim for a county batsman is to achieve 1,000 championship runs, which is generally regarded as the minimum respectable requirement for a regular player. Bowlers might want in the region of fifty or sixty wickets.

In Test cricket, a batting average of 40 has long been the accepted target – the benchmark of a fine international batsman. Anyone averaging above 50 can count themselves world-class. Don Bradman, who averaged 99.94 for Australia in fifty-two Tests between 1928 and 1948, was quite simply a batting genius. Brian Lara's first sixteen Tests put him second – and his average was 62.

Lara's determination to surpass Sir Garfield Sobers' 365 not out for the West Indies against Pakistan in Jamaica in 1957–8 – then the highest Test score in history – was at the heart of his 375 against England in Antigua thirty-six years later. Without that target constantly in his mind in the later stages of his innings, he would probably never have found the reserves of energy to achieve his feat.

The most famous target for bowlers is to become the greatest Test wicket-taker in history. When Fred Trueman set his standard of 307, Yorkshire's finest fast bowler remarked that anyone who beat him would be 'bloody tired'. But Test cricket has grown in quantity and a number of footsore bowlers have overhauled him. Kapil Dev currently holds the record with 434 Test wickets. With 131 Tests to his name, it was a record more impressive for stamina than strike rate, but that should not deflect from a magnificent feat which brought rejoicing throughout India.

U: Unorthodoxy

Throughout our cricketing life, we strive to do things by the book, learning the techniques and the principles that have evolved over many years. But players naturally blessed with a touch of the unorthodox can bring an extra dimension to the game. If something a little different regularly works for you, don't abandon it.

When Nick Knight joined Warwickshire last season, the first thing his skipper, Dermot Reeve, did was to take him into the Edgbaston indoor nets and teach him the reverse sweep. It immediately impressed upon Nick that Warwickshire players were encouraged to attempt the unconventional.

Warwickshire's determination to dictate the game, and never to shirk responsibility, has been a prime reason behind their massive success over the past two seasons. Dermot is the sort of player who infuriates the opposition – on the field, he has all manner of infuriating habits. But he is a great kidologist and is one of the finest one-day cricketers in England.

Players who strictly follow the book can become predictable. Orthodox fields can be set quite happily for a batsman unwilling to try something different. Bowlers with perfectly grooved actions have many advantages, but they are often easier to pick up as a result.

Lancashire's Neil Fairbrother is one player who it is impossible to set a field for. He is a master of the angles, working straight balls into all sorts of unlikely areas. Unorthodox but, if played with skill and precision, highly effective.

Opening batsmen are assumed to be a disciplined, safety-conscious breed: Michael Atherton and Mark Taylor, captains of England and Australia, both fit that description. But Michael Slater, Taylor's opening partner, loves to get away to a flyer. Bowlers who prefer to settle into a Test match with a few quiet maidens can be disturbed to find the game running away with them before they've time to think.

Within reason, if an unorthodox shot consistently brings you success, don't be afraid to include it in your armoury. Nigel Briers has spent the best part of twenty years at Leicestershire playing certain balls outside off-stump through the legside.

Kim Barnett, at Derbyshire, has decided that moving across his stumps as the bowler bowls has made him a more effective player. It attracted lots of criticism when he played for England, and

Craig McDermott suffered a few unorthodox blows from me on England's last tour of Australia. Here, I swing him for a legside six during the Sydney Test.

probably cost him a few Test caps. But young bowlers are often unsettled by it – and when they give him width, he is a brilliant cutter. The secret is to blank his movement out of your mind.

There are several unorthodox bowlers lurking around. At Worcestershire, both Stuart Lampitt and Gavin Haynes look as if they are bowling off the wrong foot, which can cause confusion. My Yorkshire team-mate, Craig White, jogs in like a medium-pacer, but can possess a startling turn of speed. I like to mix up my bowling with occasional off-spinners and leg-spinners. Saqlain Mushtaq, Pakistan's teenaged off-spinner, was credited in Australia last winter with a 'mystery' ball that runs straight on. It all makes him a tougher proposition.

There are some people who reckon my batting is a bit unorthodox, too. Can you imagine some of my shots in a coaching book? 'This is the swipe, this is the head-up slice.' That might cause a shock or two.

V: Visualisation

Visualisation is largely self-confidence by another name. I've never really got into it, but the Australians love it, and they are the best side in the world at the moment, so it shouldn't be dismissed out of hand.

I'm naturally a confident sort of bloke, always bursting with the belief that I'm going to do well. I don't think many of my team-mates think that my ego needs artificially boosting. But if you are the sort of player who frets about the outcome of a match, then visualisation might be just what you need.

Before every game, it is vital to banish negative thoughts from your mind. This is especially true in high-pressure matches – perhaps a cup final, or a match when promotion or relegation is at stake – when the consequences of failure can be so much higher, and so doubts can easily creep in.

Visualisation is a technique which teaches players to remain positive. Basically, it suggests that players should imagine themselves in the game they are about to play. Batsmen should visualise playing each bowler successfully, building up their confidence with a series of positive images. Bowlers might visualise a consistent over which ends with a wicket. Slip fielders might concentrate on the ball catching the edge of the bat, and travelling safely into their hands.

The intention is that players feel good about their ability, and that they do not hamstring themselves by the fear of failure. When we lose confidence, the brain can actually inhibit the body, preventing our natural talent from shining through.

Much of visualisation is really just common sense. If you are waiting to go into bat, it is obviously beneficial if you think you are going to do well. But how many times have you secretly worried that you are going to fail? Once is too often.

Sometimes I dream about cricket matches, and in nearly every case, I am successful in my dream. That, in its way, is a form of visualisation – the brain convincing itself that it can cope.

I've also been in teams that have employed a dressing-room psychologist before a match. The psychologist's job will be to trot out a few impressive phrases to encourage them to think positively, to yearn for success rather than to fear failure. Personally, I don't hold much store by it. If the psychologist hasn't seen us play, how does he know we are any good? It all seems unnatural, sitting there politely. I'd rather listen to a team-mate who knows more about me.

The last time I heard of anybody trying to explain visualisation to a local club side, they were bowled out for 70.

Exhortations to them to think positively, and have belief in themselves, were taken as a licence to try to slog nearly every ball out of the ground. The result – total disaster. It's not quite as simple as that.

But one thing is undoubtedly true. It only takes two or three pessimists in a side to dramatically reduce its effectiveness. If people do not think they can win a game, they should not be playing in the first place. Warwickshire's success over the past two English seasons has been a triumph of positive thinking. All power to them.

W: Wealth

Wealthy professional cricketers are fairly small in number, certainly in comparison with leading footballers, tennis players or golfers. But no one would deny that most of us enjoy a comfortable standard of living. Alongside that there is a charm to the life that makes it an immensely worthwhile career for anyone with the talent and the aptitude to succeed.

I've always believed that prosperity is as much to do with quality of life as money. The chance to play a game I enjoy – rather than be stuck in a boring job, watching the clock and just waiting for the weekend – is something I should be thankful for. But professional cricketers would be foolish if they didn't recognise the shortness of their career and try to take full financial advantage before their retirement.

Cricket is my job and, like most other people, I want to get to the top of the tree and stay there – and to enjoy the financial rewards that my success will bring. I can expect a professional career of about fifteen years, barring serious injury, so it's important that I do everything to secure the future of myself and my family. To have no idea of your employment prospects at thirty-five can be unnerving.

That is why my various sponsorships, outside cricket, are so vital. I've been lucky to endorse a limited number of high-quality products: contracts, for instance, with Pony, Duncan Fearnley, Scottish Life, Oakley and Nivea Sun. Most importantly, none of my outside commitments has ever been allowed to affect my cricket. Becoming sidetracked by outside interests is the stupidest mistake a sportsman can make.

County cricket's benefit system is also regarded by some critics as being outdated. The argument is that some professionals hang on for a benefit year (normally given after about ten years as a capped player) when their enthusiasm for the game has long diminished. This, in turn, makes it harder for young players to break into the side.

It is hard to justify the fairness of a system when one player earns, say, £100,000 from a benefit year and a player of similar ability and record is sacked only a year before his benefit is due. This sort of thing happens all the time. The player fortunate enough to get the benefit gains financial security; the one who doesn't might reach thirty with little money and few prospects. But unless county salaries rise considerably, or pension schemes are properly introduced, the benefit system will be defended to the hilt.

Most county cricketers are only employed for six months of the year, from April to September. Many grab winter jobs wherever they can, and many others have no choice but to sign on the dole in the off-season. For a fit, young sportsman, used to daily activity, it can be a frustrating time. The Cricketers' Association is gradually winning the argument that more county players should be actively involved in coaching in schools and clubs. Just imagine how that might improve your own game.

X: Xystus

A covered terrace used by athletes in Ancient Greece for gentle exercise. Things have certainly become more demanding since then! (Well, what would you have thought of?)

Y: Youth

When England are in trouble, they turn to experience. When Australia are struggling, they turn to youth. You can always find exceptions, but generally speaking that is the greatest difference in attitudes between the two countries.

Many Australians were amused by our decision to include Graham Gooch and Mike Gatting on the last Ashes tour. They shared our respect for two fine Test players, but thought that only England could have planned to combat Shane Warne with such experience, rather than put their faith in the dash and flair of younger players. By the end of the tour, both Goochie and Gatt had retired from Test cricket. Australians were even more amazed when England recalled forty-two-year-old Colin Cowdrey to face the searing pace of Lillee and Thomson in 1974–5.

Young Australian players are deliberately put under pressure, in the belief that the toughest will survive. If some players fall by the wayside, then that is the price that has to be paid. They would probably never be mentally tough enough to succeed at the highest level.

In England, we tend to treat young players with more compassion. We are more wary of making excessive demands in case we wreck a youngster's enthusiasm for playing cricket. Players will develop in their own time, we tend to say. Nurture them carefully.

Whatever the respective merits of both systems, there is no doubt that Australian players develop much more quickly than ours. They often grow up much faster and have a brasher, more aggressive approach to life. They are encouraged to play their cricket in a forceful, assertive fashion.

In England, young players showing too much on-field aggression are liable to incur the displeasure of teachers, coaches or the opposition. They might gain a reputation for being troublesome and find that their cricketing opportunities are reduced as a result. We are determined to educate our young players to play the game in the proper spirit. That is important, but the danger is that we become too soft. More than 10,000 overseas players visited England last summer, most of them teenagers mixing some cricket with a chance for an extended holiday, and a chance to travel. Many are Australians, and many of them shock our own cricketers with the self-assertive way that they play the game. Their cricketing upbringing has been different.

I'm not recommending the Australian way entirely. I'm also convinced that there is no reason why English cricket should not be the best in the world. But, as a young player learning the game in England, it is easy to take the comfortable option, and not to push yourself hard enough in your early years. Sometimes, you might even feel that it's not very cool to try so hard. Tell that to an Aussie. They think it's not very cool to lose.

Z: Zzzzz

Get plenty of sleep. Good night.

Index